Kurhessische Landeszeitung

Die parteiamtliche Tageszeitung des Gaues Kurhessen der NSDAP / Gauorgan der DAF Gau Kurhessen

Hessische Volkswacht / Gemeinnutz geht vor Eigennutz!

Einzelpreis 10 Pfg.

Nr. 194.

Kassel, Donnerstag, 20. August 1942

13. Jahrgang

Englisches Expeditionskorps erlitt bei Dieppe katastrophale Niederlage

...nsversuch gescheitert

...hohen blutigen Verlusten für den Gegner zusammengebrochen / ...Festland / Großer Erfolg unseres Küstenschutzes / Seit 16 Uhr kein Einsatz von Reserven unnötig

M-Stammlager IX C
Bad Sulza (Thür.)

...es Fiasko

Flakkreuzer „Cairo" und Zerstörer „Foresight" versenkt

Ticket to Hell
via Dieppe

FROM A PRISONER'S WARTIME LOG 1942-1945

This narrative is dedicated to my dear wife and family, and I gratefully acknowledge the assistance of my daughter, Lynda, in its preparation.
Also, a very special 'thank you' to the Canadian and International Red Cross.

Ticket to Hell
via Dieppe

FROM A PRISONER'S WARTIME LOG 1942–1945

A. Robert Prouse

Van Nostrand Reinhold

Toronto   New York

Published in 1982 by
Van Nostrand Reinhold Publishers
A Division of International Thomson Limited
1410 Birchmount Road
Scarborough, Ontario, Canada M1P 2E7

Canadian Cataloguing in Publication Data
Prouse, A. Robert (Arthur Robert), 1911–
   Ticket to hell via Dieppe

ISBN 0-7706-0009-3

1. World War, 1939–1945—Prisoners and prisons, German. 2. World War, 1939–1945—Personal narratives, Canadian. 3. Prouse, A. Robert (Arthur Robert), 1911–   4. Stalag IXC (Bad Sulza, Germany: Concentration camp). 5. Prisoners of war—Germany—Biography. 6. Prisoners of war—Canada—Biography. I. Title.
D895.G3P76   940.54'72'43220924   C81-095107-X

A co-publication of Van Nostrand Reinhold Publishers, Toronto and Webb & Bower (Publishers) Limited, Exeter

Designed by Malcolm Couch
Typeset in Great Britain by August Filmsetting, Warrington, Cheshire

Printed and bound in Great Britain by the Fakenham Press, Norfolk

82 83 84 85 86 87 88   7 6 5 4 3 2 1

Contents

Prologue

When war was declared in September, 1939, I wanted to join the army. I had always loved everything military and, as a child, had read and reread exciting stories of the First World War. I was eager to enter this new war and realize my childhood dreams of battle and glory. My wife of three months took a dim view of this desire, however, so I stayed on at her brother's farm in St Felix de Valois, tending chickens in the summer and cutting logs in the winter.

In early spring of 1940 I headed back to Montreal to resume my work as a freelance investigator, a field I had gone into after spending the worst of the Depression years going from road crew jobs to railroad construction gangs to working in the gold mines of Val d'Or, Quebec. After a few weeks I tried to join the RCMP but my married status ruled me out. I then presented myself in April, 1940, at Place Viger barracks and enlisted in the Canadian Provost Corps. They were looking for men with investigative experience and they assured me that the outfit would soon be going to England.

I returned home in uniform and very nearly broke up a perfect marriage.

Two months later, on the date of my first wedding anniversary, I prepared to leave Halifax aboard the *Duchess of Athol*. I missed my wife terribly and the empty feeling in the pit of my stomach was intensified as we pulled away from the dock but I knew it was a compulsion, no, more of an obsession, that had brought me to this point in life.

We were soon at sea, escorted by planes and corvettes, with the destroyer *Revenge* riding herd. The trip was fairly uneventful, with only one submarine scare during which depth charges were dropped by one of our escorts. I saw my first whale and heard Lord Haw Haw on the radio advising one and all that our ship, the *Duchess of Athol*, had gone down with all troops on board. This was our introduction to propaganda.

We sailed a zig-zag course, coming close to Iceland. The trip seemed endless but eventually the coast of Ireland appeared in the distance and at last we sighted a balloon barrage floating over Liverpool to protect the city from low-flying German planes.

The next two years were a mixture of excitement and extreme loneliness. My main interest in those days revolved around my motorbikes—a 'snortin Norton' and eventually a 'Harley'.

We had two months of fast training in Aldershot, which included drill, map reading, arms training and motorcycle riding, and then headed for Walton-on-the-Hill to relieve the RCMP (No 1 Cdn Provost Corps) at 7th Corps HQ near Leatherhead.

This was an exciting period, racing around the countryside on our Iron Steeds, rounding up parachutists and having a grandstand seat at the Battle of Britain. The heavy bombing went on day and night and the dogfights were a daily occurrence which held a fascination for us all. The whole thing was scary yet exciting and when we moved back to Aldershot to rejoin our division, which had now arrived in England, we missed the excitement, the near-misses of falling bombs, the general feeling of being part of the action.

The next year and a half was spent in almost constant man-oeuvres and it was not until we moved to the coastal towns of Eastbourne and Brighton that the excitement of action returned with the hit-and-run daily raids of bombing and machine-gunning.

Apart from manoeuvres, our time was filled with foot and road patrols, breaking up fights at pub closing time and, in my case, investigating everything from petty theft and assault to rape and murder. One of the more pleasant assignments was being chosen for motorcycle escort for visiting 'brass'. My personal escort duties ranged from assorted generals to Princess Patricia (Lady Patricia Ramsay), Prime Minister Churchill and the King and Queen. On Churchill's escort I picked up every cigar butt he discarded and sold them for ten shillings each, keeping one as a souvenir.

Like every other Canadian soldier, I was bored to tears with the long inaction and was itching for battle. When, in the late summer of 1942, we returned to the mainland from the Isle of Wight, where the 2nd Canadian Division had undergone intensive commando training and beach landing techniques, I was thoroughly browned off. I had missed the training due to an overload of investigative assignments. I requested a transfer back to the depot with the idea of joining a parachute corps.

Within the week, I was summoned before the CO and advised that I was due to be sent on an officers' training course but that, since I had been bitching about inaction, he would offer me a choice—OTC or going on what he called 'a special manoeuvre'. I chose the latter and within a few days was seated in a truck headed for the coast with other members of our company, the No 2 Canadian Provost Corps.

1: A Raid on Dieppe

Attempted Invasion Has Collapsed

SPECIAL COMMUNIQUÉ

From the Führer's Headquarters, Aug. 19th, 1942.

A large-scale landing of British, American, Canadian and de Gaulist troops, the first wave of which was about one division strong, which was carried out early this morning on the French Channel coast near Dieppe, under cover of strong naval and air forces, and supported by tanks, has been repulsed by the German coastal defence forces, the enemy sustaining heavy losses in dead and wounded. Mopping-up operations were finished by four o'clock this afternoon.

This great success was achieved without any of the reserves at the disposal of the higher command having to be brought into action.

As becomes evident from reports from the troops concerned and from statements made by prisoners, the landing operations took the following course:

The first wave of landing troops was transferred early this morning from transports at sea to 300 to 400 landing-boats and reached the coast at five minutes past six o'clock, pro-

tected by 13 to 15 cruisers and destroyers, as well as strong fighter forces. Behind these stood a reserve of 6 transports and 3 freighters and further north a group of 26 transports as operational reserve. This probably represented the bulk of the landing forces. These were to be brought into action as soon as the first wave of landing troops had succeeded in forming a bridgehead round the harbour of Dieppe.

This stage was never reached The enemy as far as he had landed was wiped out in close-range fighting and thrown into the sea. Of tanks which had been landed and were destroyed later 28 have been counted so far.

More than 1500 prisoners, amongst them 60 Canadian officers, are in German hands. The casualties of the enemy are extremely high.

3 destroyers, 2 torpedo-boats and 2 transports were sunk by artillery fire. The Luftwaffe shot down 83 enemy aircraft, sank 2 special troops-transports and one E-Boat and damaged 5 cruisers or large destroyers as well as 2 transports by heavy bomb hits.

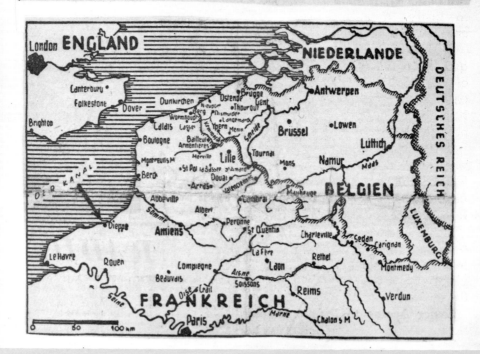

The report in the POW newspaper *The Camp* carried the German propaganda that the raid on Dieppe was in fact an invasion.

CHAPTER 1

A Raid on Dieppe

After a brief and uneventful journey, we arrived in Portsmouth and immediately were loaded on tank landing craft. Notepaper was issued on which to write our last letters home and, shortly after, we received our Sten machine guns. The landing craft headed slowly out into the choppy waters of the Channel and only then were we advised of our mission—a raid on Dieppe.

There was a beautiful sunset as we sailed along the coast and my thoughts were a mixture of what tomorrow would bring and what had happened during the two years since enlisting. As the dark of night settled like a shroud, my thoughts also turned to home and my wife of such a short time. I felt a deep longing to be safely in her arms, away from this alien setting and the unbearable feeling of loneliness that had wrapped itself around me. I was surrounded by others in a like predicament, yet I felt so alone.

I tried to shake the feeling as I spread my ground sheet underneath a Churchill tank on Landing Craft No 5. I lay down, pulled my blanket around my ears, settled my head on my steel helmet and immediately fell into a deep sleep.

I was rudely awakened by the stacatto sound of gunfire and quickly scrambled from beneath the tank, clambering up the side of the boat to get a better look at what was going on. It was almost 04:00 and the night was blacker than the hubs of hell, but this only heightened the glow of the tracer bullets that filled the air. It was beautiful to watch, something like a July 1st fireworks display, but it was also strangely awesome, especially as we didn't know what was going on and couldn't do much about it anyway. Later we learned that we had run into a German convoy, which eventually broke away from the action and no doubt warned the German forces ashore of what was coming in.

It was August 19, 1942. The dawn broke and we sighted the coastline of France. Directly in front of us was the sleepy seaside town of Dieppe. The outlines of buildings were becoming dimly visible, particularly a large structure that was our destination and that we later learned was the casino.

Suddenly all hell broke loose. The air was filled with the hum of bullets sounding like a swarm of angry bees. Mortar shells were exploding all around us and Stuka bombers dive-bombed to beat hell. As we drew closer to the shore the navy gunner who had been handling the Bofors gun suddenly disappeared in a puff of smoke. When it cleared, I could see the gun still in place and couldn't understand what had happened. The dead man was quickly replaced and the firing continued. As the ramp of our landing craft was lowered at about 05:40, the men in the front row started to fall. Others, myself included, tried to hug the side of the craft. We could see that these bastards weren't fooling.

Finally, I got tired of being a sitting duck and ran to the front, stepping over all the bodies. I jumped into the sea yelling, 'Let's get the hell out of here.' I was up to my thighs in the water and still don't know how I got ashore without being hit. I threw my body on to the coarse gravel beach and squirmed my way towards the concrete sea wall. I had to get through a mess of barbed wire already strewn with bodies and finally pulled myself up to the wall where a soldier lay dead, draped over the barbed wire that ran along the top. Carefully I raised my head to try and see what was happening on the other side of the wall but quickly withdrew it, for it seemed that the whole German army was shooting at me personally.

I could see that some of the tanks had made it to shore and were churning up the gravel. They would turn and fire, then head up the beach a few yards and repeat the procedure. One tried to breach the wall but the tracks spun on the concrete as it tried to climb at a dangerous angle. It finally gave up and backed onto the beach, repeating its fire-and-spin technique.

I made my way to a burning scout car, which afforded some protection. I flopped down behind it and found three or four men from our company. Scanning the beach from right to left, all I could see were prone bodies. I was unable to tell the dead from the living, as everyone was hugging the ground. Heavy fire continued to come from all directions at once, making it impossible to group and form some plan of action.

Looking out over the water, I could see our navy bombarding the town and could hear the whistle of shells going over our heads. This was great but it did not cause any lull in the heavy fire that rained down on the beach. What we needed was air support, a heavy bombing to silence some of the guns and allow us to move into town with at least some chance of survival.

One of the men in our small group had a ball through his shoulder and was having a difficult time moving. Every time a tank came roaring down the beach, I would have to grab my buddy by the heels and pull him away from the grinding tracks. On one of these occasions, I spotted an apparently dead soldier who lay on his back with his knees up in the air. One leg had been half blown off. Except for this, he appeared to be enjoying the August sunshine. I noticed that, instead of the khaki issue shirt, he was wearing a bright green sweater. As I took in this scene, a tank bore down on him and after passing, all I could see was a misshapen red form with bits of bright green intermingled. I found myself wondering who he was, what part of Canada had he come from, did his wife or mother know at that moment that they would never see him again?

I didn't have much time to dwell on the subject. There was a blinding explosion as a mortar shell hit the scout car. All I could feel was a numbing sensation in my legs as shrapnel entered my flesh. As the smoke cleared, I adjusted the steel helmet that had been knocked down over my eyes. Four of my fingers went through a hole that had been blown in it and for a moment I panicked and tore off the helmet to feel my head, fully expecting my hands to come away covered with blood. There wasn't even a scratch. At that moment I fully appreciated this object that I had always disliked and usually referred to disdainfully as 'my God-damned tin hat'.

After muttering a silent prayer of thanks, I looked to the others, who had all been hit with shrapnel as I had. One had blood spurting from beneath his armpit and asked me to bandage him. I advised him and the others to make their way to a beached craft, where they could take shelter, since first I had to take care of my buddy with the ball in his shoulder. When I turned to help him, I couldn't believe my eyes. He had completely disappeared. (Fear must have lent wings to his feet, as he did survive. We met later in Germany.)

I looked towards the beached craft to see if the men had made it. Evidently they had, since no one was in sight except the one with the arm wound. Instead of heading for the craft, he had run wildly into the water. As I watched, he was hit by a wave and momentarily disappeared; then I caught sight of him flailing his arms and swimming madly out to sea. (Years later, I learned that he had eventually been picked up and actually got back to England.)

I started to work my way toward the beached craft, first crawling on my stomach, then running in a zig-zag path until I felt another piece of shrapnel hit my foot. The rest of the way, I stayed on my stomach. When finally I got behind the craft, I was surprised by the number of soldiers who were grouped there. Then I realized that it was the only protection on the beach, having swung side-

öllig zerschlagen, sie retteten nur das nackte Le-
en. PK-Aufn.: Kriegsberichter Antonowitz - HH.

So endete Churchills zweite Front bei Dieppe.
PK-Aufn.: Kriegsberichter Treff-Atlan

id Landungsboote; rechts: Gefallene Briten und vernichtete Panzer
; PK-Kriegsberichter Meyer-Wittenberger (Wb.) (2). PK-Kriegsberichter Koll-Atlanti

ngsversuch. Links und Mitte: **Zerschossene Panzer u**
PK.-Kriegsberichter Ko

Der Strand von Dieppe nach dem gescheiterten britischen Land

Left : The beach was littered with corpses. Many men never made it beyond the tangle of barbed wire on the sea wall. Others stripped off their clothes in their attempts to swim to freedom and were captured, embarrassingly, without their trousers.

Above : Thirty-three landing craft, including No. 5, my transport across the Channel, were casualties of the raid. Every tank that landed was stranded on the stony beach.

ways, knocked there by the waves after being put out of commission.

Up to this moment, I had felt no fear but, as I sank to my knees, I started to shake and began to tear at the gravel with both hands with the idea of digging myself underground. All of a sudden I realized what I was doing and came to my senses. I then relaxed for the first time since landing and knew that for all of us this had been much too explosive for our first time in action. I tried to imagine what the others, who hadn't come with us on the raid, were doing. I pictured them sitting in some pub, having a cool beer and shooting the breeze.

After a period of day-dreaming, I stood up and started to take stock of what was happening. A soldier beside me stepped partly out of the craft's protection. I told him to be careful but he just said, 'To hell with the bastards!' He had hardly got the words out when I heard him gasp, 'Oh Christ!' His face was ashen as he grabbed at his stomach and tried desperately to push back his insides. As he fell dead, everything seemed to pop out in a stream of crimson. I hugged the craft as close as possible. It was a comforting feeling.

I gradually became aware of a familiar drone and looked skywards. For the first time since landing, I could see a squadron of Spitfires heading our way. They peeled off and took after the Stukas and in nothing flat, two of the German dive bombers were hit and started to fall with black smoke pouring from them. One dived into the sea, while the other came down in a slow circle. Two men fell from this plane, their chutes billowing out above them. One landed in the sea directly in front of us and started to swim to shore after getting rid of his chute. As he emerged from the water, I could see his pale and panic-stricken face. It seemed whiter than the shirt he was wearing and his whole body shook with cold and fear. One of the soldiers raised his rifle and said, 'I'm going to kill the bastard', but two of us knocked the rifle down and reminded the hot-head that the Jerry was unarmed and had his hands above his head in surrender. The flyer stumbled ashore, fell exhausted at our feet and lay there with no further attention being paid to him.

At about this time, around 11:00, we heard a shout from the beachmaster and suddenly realized that planes were approaching very low and laying a smoke screen over our heads. We then became aware that the LCTs were approaching to try to evacuate us. They came rushing in with their front ramps dropping, not coming too close because of the heavy gunfire. As soon as they reached a certain point we could hear the roar of the reversed engines as they started to move backwards very slowly. The troops ran into the sea in a mad scramble, trying their damnedest somehow to board the craft and escape this hell. Men were mowed down by machine-gun fire. The LCT directly in front of where I was standing received a direct hit from a bomb that had been dropped by one of the dive bombers. All around me, arms, legs and bits of what had been brave men flew into the air. In the lulls between explosions, I could hear the screams of the badly wounded. Many craft lay crippled and sinking but others still approached, manned by gallant navy men who seemed to disregard the screaming lead that was hurtling in their direction.

I decided that if ever I was going to make a move now was the time. The smoke screen was lifting and no more planes were approaching to lay more smoke. I left my weapons on shore and ran into the sea. The surface ahead of me was so heavily sprayed by machine-gun bullets that it appeared as if a downpour of rain had hit the area, an impossibility on a brilliantly sunny day. The craft I had been heading for was suddenly hit and started to burn. I could hear the constant whistle of bullets and wondered why I too had not been hit. I decided not to tempt fate any longer and dived under the surface, turned, and headed back to shore to the protection of the beached LCT.

As I stood there, watching the carnage, I could feel the sea gently nudging my legs as the tide came in. It was then that I realized that the water was no longer green but an angry red, stained by the blood of the dead and dying. Bodies floated over the surface and, as the tide swelled higher, they washed against me in the ebb and flow. I looked at them and felt a terrible sorrow, not just for them but for those that would vainly await their return.

I felt no fear because I wasn't there at that moment. I was detached from the whole bloody scene, watching the tragedy from afar. I was a silent spectator at a mass sea burial. This state of mind seemed to last for some time, as I floated above it all, taking in every minute detail. I came back to reality with a shudder. I gazed down at the dead soldier who was bumping against my legs. He was face up and his lids were rolled back, showing only the whites of his eyes. I thought those lids were fluttering, trying to tell me something, but all I could do was stare in a dreadful fascination.

Slowly, I became aware that a deathly silence had settled over

The Camp

ILLUSTRATED WEEKLY

No 112   BERLIN   SEPTEMBER 6, 1942

First aid for wounded British soldiers

Weekly Military Survey

THE EASTERN FRONT

The battles on the Eastern Front have brought further successes to German arms. The drive is continuing in the south of the front despite the fact that enemy defensive operations are assisted by natural obstacles to the German advance. After the announcement on the 25th August that the German war flag had already been waving for some days on the Elbrus, the highest peak of the Caucasus range, the army report repeatedly referred to high mountain passes and enemy nests in the mountains, which were wrested from the Soviets after heavy fighting. In the same way the drive to the south of the lower Kuban is making further progress in the teeth of stubborn enemy resistance and despite difficult terrain. Rumanian troops are adding to their laurels here as well.

The battle of Stalingrad is increasing in intensity. After German troops had succeeded in crossing the Don in large numbers opposite Stalingrad the attack was pushed forward towards the city from a westerly direction. The fortress of Stalingrad is being stubbornly defended by the enemy from strongly fortified positions. It was announced on the 31st August that German troops had broken through the defences south of Stalingrad and are now only 25 km. to the south of the city. The Luftwaffe is rendering excellent assistance in the attack on the city, having inflicted heavy losses on the enemy during day and night operations.

With regard to the Soviet attempt to break through the German positions with strong forces in the Don sector, the report of the German Supreme Command contains a summary covering the period of time from the 20th July. The enemy has cast the enemy enormous losses in men and material. Since the 20th July, in this area and in this figure has since been increased by a further 48, 547 aircraft have been brought down, our own losses being 25. The losses of Soviet man power are stated to have been extraordinarily high. Similar attempts to cause withdrawals of German troops from the southern front were made by the enemy in the Kaluga sector to the south of Lake Ladoga and, to a lesser extent, in the Leningrad area. All these attempts ended in failure since all the attacks collapsed in face of the German defences. They resulted in the enemy losing 157 panzers in addition to those mentioned above. The losses of the Soviet air force have again been very high. From the 1st to the 24th August they totalled 2505. The enemy lost 153 planes on the 25th and 26th August alone. In connection with the splendid achievement of the Luftwaffe mention should be made of Major Gollob, Commodore of a fighter squadron, who gained his 150th air victory.

THE WAR IN THE AIR

In addition to the above successes of the Luftwaffe on the Eastern Front our units gained further laurels in defensive operations against British raiders, and on raids on targets in Britain. Enemy raids on occupied territory in the west and over Germany proved very costly for the British. The damage they caused to property and the attendant civilian casualties cost them 128 planes during the period under review. For purposes of comparison it may be added that from the 14th—27th August the British lost 315 planes in the West as against 63 German machines. The reports of the German Supreme Command daily contain references to German raids against industrial targets and supply depots in all parts of Britain. Shipping along the Channel coast has also been attacked. A British merchantman of 5,000 tons and an escort vessel were sunk.

THE WAR AT SEA

The enemy hope that a drop in shipping losses would follow the defensive measures adopted against the U-Boats was not to be fulfilled. The Special Bulletin of the 31st August announced that in the Atlantic, the Caribbean Sea, and off the West African coast, that is along the important Anglo-American shipping routes, 30 ships with 181,000 tons have been sunk from convoys and by independent actions. A further 5 ships were torpedoed. Patrol craft of the German Navy succeeded in sinking an enemy submarine in the North Sea.

WORLD AND WAR NEWS

The Führer has nominated the President of the People's Court, Dr Thierack (formerly Secretary of State) Minister for Justice and has bestowed upon him special powers.

Herr v. Papen to Budapest as representative of the Führer at the obsequies of Stefan v. Horthy. Field-Marshall, General Keitel was also a member of the special delegation that accompanied Herr v. Ribbentrop.

Throughout the whole of Ireland meetings and demonstrations of various kinds are being held with the object of urging a reprieve by the British authorities for the six members of the I.R.A. recently condemned to death.

The Council of People's Commissars in the Union has nominated General Shukov Deputy People's Commissar for Defence.

According to a report from London the Soviet troops in Iran and Iraq are to be placed in a new Command under General Quinan-Wilson. These troops were formerly under the Command of General Wavell in India.

It is reported from Teheran that the Iranian Minister of the Interior has resigned from office in consequence of difficulties that have arisen between him and the Bolshevik Ambassador.

The state of military law existing in Iran has been intensified.

Reports from Bagdad state that 25 officers of the Iraq army and a government official have been arrested by the British.

The Turkish President, M. Inönü, has arrived in the coastal district of the Black Sea during a journey of inspection through central Anatolia.

British military authorities in Egypt have arrested Prince Abbas Halim and the leader of the Egyptian Labour Party, Muhammed Tahel Pasha.

Negro trade-unions in South Africa have been recognized unreservedly.

Martial Law has been proclaimed in the Indian province of Orissa.

The Government of Madras has announced that it is in possession of positive information

Mr. Oliver Lyttelton, Minister of Production, informed the people of the U.S.A. in a broadcast that Great Britain produces in proportion to its population twice as much war material as the United States.

The "Times" states that the battle of the West Atlantic is for the Allies one of the climacterics of the war.

Lord Moyne has been appointed Deputy Secretary of State and is to render assistance to Mr. Casey, the Australian, in his capacity of Minister of State in the Middle East.

The Special Correspondent of the "Sunday Times" reports from Moscow that the Soviets are "very astonished" at the frustrated attempt of invasion at Dieppe, at the strength of the German resistance and at the high losses of the Allies.

to the effect that the Working Comittee of the All Indian Congress has issued instructions for the campaign of civil disobedience to be put into operation.

New serious rioting is reported from Bombay, Calcutta and Madras.

The position in India has caused Chang Kai Chek to warn, in a long message, the small bodies of Chinese troops that have remained in India against participating in the internal affairs of India or passing criticism on Britain's Indian policy.

The Burmese Volunteer Corps, that distinguished itself in the defence of Burma, has been reorganised into a "Burmese Defence Army."

According to official Japanese reports a second naval battle has developed off the Solomon Islands.

The study of Japanese has been made obligatory in all foreign and Chinese schools in Shanghai. This regulation affects more than 240,000 scholars.

Mr. Frazer, Prime Minister of New Zealand has arrived at Roosevelt's invitation on a visit to the U.S.A.

The President of the U.S.A. has invited Mr. Curtin, Prime Minister of Australia, and General Smuts to visit him in the United States during the course of the year.

Roosevelt received the British Ambassador, Lord Halifax, during his stay on the Tuesday the 25th August.

Mr. Churchill has recently died of wounds following his return from London, where he held positions in the Middle East, in India and and Mr. Churchill's trip to Moscow.

Sir John is the most prominent military representative of Britain in the United States, has returned by air to England.

Rear-Admiral Dorling of the Department of Supplies in the U.S. Admiralty stated in an interview that only surface craft can transport the millions of tons of supplies needed for the soldiers of the allied nations. They cannot be replaced by cargo planes.

Roosevelt has announced the introduction of a control on the cost of living. This will be effected in conjunction with a stabilization of agricultural prices.

Mr. Nelson, Chief of the U.S. War Production Board, declared on accepting the resignation of the President of the Iron and Steel Board that he will henceforth be compelled to adopt a more rigorous and realistic attitude with regard to the release of raw materials for purposes unconnected with the war effort.

The "New York Daily Mirror" asserts that the general assumption of American participation at Dieppe is not founded on fact. The part played by U.S. troops was insignificant.

Mr. Hull, U.S. Foreign Minister, has made an announcement concerning "part-agreements of a commercial and political nature" between the U.S.A. and Portugal. He was unable to state, however, to what extent these refer to the Portuguese colonies.

Referring to the clamour for a Second Front the U.S. periodical "Time" states that there are quite enough fronts which cannot be adequately provided with troops and war material.

Bolshevik students have arrived in Washington to participate in an international Students' Conference.

Mr. Mackenzie King, the Canadian Prime Minister, has announced the establishment of a Bureau of War Information.

The Bolivian Minister of Foreign Affairs has resigned.

New trade pacts have been signed between Spain and the Argentine, whereby Spain is to receive meat and grain in exchange for iron, olive-oil and preserved fish.

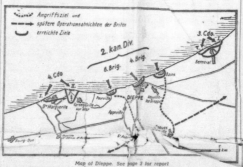

Angriffsziel und *spätere Operationsabsichten der Briten erreichte Ziele*

Map of Dieppe. See page 2 for report

HOME NEWS IN BRIEF

According to statistics published by the Ministry of Labour the average wages of workers have risen by 46 % since 1938, whilst the cost of living has increased by 26 %. The standard of living of the workers is thus higher than before the war.

Sir Horace Wilson, Permanent Under Secretary for State to the Treasury and Head of the Civil Service has resigned.

The President of the British Spa Committee, Lord Kimberley, warned the public on the occasion of a speech in Manchester that they would be better advised in increasing their contributions towards the war than in perpetually clamouring for a second front.

The "Daily Herald" criticizes the reportage of Mr. Bracken, Minister of Information regarding Churchill's Moscow trip. The Prime Minister's appearance in an airforce uniform with a white umbrella was especially mentioned.

The British Transport and Factory Worker's Union reports that its membership has now reached the million mark, and that it is therefore the largest Try to union in the world.

From next week to the end of October the allocation of milk for consumers not entitled to rations will average 3 pints a week.

British breweries are suggesting to licensing authorities that a rationing of beer should be introduced. This could be effected by closing public house 4 days a week.

Arms workers from London who have been compelled to work in Manchester have gone on strike on account of the bad working conditions there.

Textile distribution in Britain has been cut down. The 60 points which during the past year covered 12 months have now been extended for 14 months.

The "Evening Standard" of the 20th August complains of propaganda activity following the Dieppe expedition. For 24 hours after the conclusion of the operations not even a correspondent's report was available for the evening papers, although no fewer than 22 reporters and wireless speakers had participated. Lord Mountbatten's headquarters released eye-witness accounts as early as midday but the censor in the Ministry of Information was still examining them late that night.

The British General Council of Trade-Unions declared that the negotiations of Sir Walter Citrine, the General Secretary, with the workers' organisations in the U.S.A. have failed completely.

Government has raised the ban on the "Daily Thread" on the periodical 'The Week'.

C. Whit...
C.P. w the Minister of Labour, and Mr. Alexander, ..5th ord of the Admiralty, have had discussions...
Pte F..th representatives of the shipping industry.
D. dock workers concerning the serious..
Pte J.shipping.
Pte Ste- ...
Pte G. s
Pte B.
Your Deputy Head of the Imperial General General Hugh Royds Stokes Massy has d.

Above : Wounded soldiers rested in front of the Dieppe hospital awaiting their orders to march (in the case of the walking wounded) or their transport to other medical centres.

Left : The map reproduced in *The Camp* was an accurate rendering of the battle plan, copies of which were captured by the Germans.

the beach. No more boats approached and all I could see in the distance was the smoke from the funnels of the navy vessels as they returned to England. I realized it was all over as the beachmaster shouted instructions for everyone to throw their arms into the sea and get rid of all identification. After this order was carried out, a soldier stepped out from behind our craft waving a white hand-kerchief. A shot rang out and he dropped from sight. The German airman who had been completely forgotten was now pushed to the front and, with hands raised high and his whole body shaking with terror, he was forced to move out from behind our protective shield. The Germans must have recognized him immediately as one of their own, for there were no more shots and we could hear the guttural shouts ordering us to come out and surrender. We emerged one by one and I was amazed at how close the enemy had been, with just the LCT separating us.

It was about half past one on a sunny afternoon, and for us the war was over.

2: Limping Towards Germany

A PHOTOSTAT COPY OF A CANADIAN 2ND DIV. ORDER, SIGNED BY CAPT. EISINGER AND FOUND ON A CANADIAN OFFICER WHEN CAPTURED AT DIEPPE, AUG. 19, 1942, WAS PUBLISHED, AND A COPY POSTED ON ALL PRISONER OF WAR CAMPS - ORDER BOARDS THROUGHOUT GERMANY. IT STATED IN SHORT —

"A PRISONER OF WAR CAGE WILL BE ESTABLISHED AT — "
"ALL GERMAN P.O.W. WILL BE ASSEMBLED THERE, FOR SEARCHING AND INTERROGATION BY THE CANADIAN PROVOST CORPS."
"THEIR HANDS SHOULD BE TIED BEHIND THEIR BACKS TO PREVENT THEIR DESTROYING OF ANY DOCUMENTS, MAPS, ETC. IN THEIR POSSESSION." ETC. ETC.

(THE ABOVE ORDER WAS GIVEN AS THE REASON, FOR THE GERMAN REPRISAL, OF CHAINING ALL CANADIANS)

NOTE - THIS 'RAID', WAS STATED BY THE GERMAN MILITARY H.Q., TO BE "AN ATTEMPTED SECOND FRONT."

CONTRARY TO THIS WAS THE LEAFLETS THAT WERE PRINTED FOR THE FRENCH CIVIL POPULATION OF DIEPPE - IN SHORT IT READ :—
"KEEP UNDER COVER AND DO NOT TRY TO ASSIST OUR TROOPS IN ANY WAY. THIS IS NOT AN INVASION BUT A 'COUP DE MAIN'"

The directive to tie POWs' hands was contrary to the Geneva Conventions. Canadians captured at Dieppe and sent directly to camps were shackled every day for months.

CHAPTER 2

Limping Towards Germany

There were long lines of Germans standing with fixed bayonets waiting to welcome us to this seaside resort. They were yelling and motioning us to put our hands on the tops of our heads. As my eyes wandered down the lines, what struck me as odd was that there wasn't one Jerry whose lips weren't trembling. Maybe, like us, it was their first time to meet the enemy face to face. I don't know why, but at that moment I felt that we were the victors and they the defeated.

I also felt deeply disappointed that in only a few hours of hell and frustration all of my boyhood dreams of reliving Ypres, Mons and other great battles had been wiped out in one fell swoop. I tried to think of what else could have been done to change this defeat into victory and came to a personal conclusion that the difference was the lack of fire power that should have been laid down ahead of us. This would have enabled the troops to advance instead of being pinned down on the beach. The navy and our fighter planes did their best but we had needed a pre-invasion bombardment and continuous air support. To this day I believe this could have turned the tide in our favour.

All these thoughts, feelings and impressions jostled in my mind as we were marched through the German lines in single file. Our helmets were collected and thrown in a pile, no doubt to be melted down and turned into shrapnel. Next, we had to empty our pockets and we watched as they greedily grabbed our watches and lighters, disregarding our money. One soldier screamed at me, motioning toward my empty holster. The shape of the .38 was still visible. I had to unbuckle and drop it before he prodded me on with his rifle butt.

We were marched through Dieppe, which in parts was reduced to rubble, and French civilians scrambled from air raid shelters to give us the 'V' for victory sign. It was a nice gesture and a hopeful sign for the future but they were soon chased away. We arrived in front of a hospital, where our captors separated the badly wounded from the walking wounded. I joined the latter and, as we stood in the hot sun, I suddenly blacked out—most likely a delayed reaction to the tensions, from our dawn landing to our mid-afternoon surrender. When I came to, I saw a nurse bending over me. She looked kind and considerate, so it didn't make any difference that I couldn't understand what she was saying.

When I got to my feet, the column of walking wounded had left and I had missed going with most of my friends. Some of the more seriously wounded were carried into the Dieppe hospital but, as there was still some air activity, most of us were loaded into box-cars and transported to a hospital in Rouen-sur-Seine, where all I can remember is being put to bed and sleeping solidly until the following morning.

On awakening, I tried to swing my legs over the side of the bed but all they did was to flop like two dead lumps of meat. I was scared to beat hell, as every time I attempted to get up, my legs would collapse. I rubbed them furiously, trying to get some life back into them. After about fifteen minutes and with the help of the soldier in the next bed, I finally felt some life in them. The colour slowly started to come back and, gradually, so did the feeling. They hurt like hell but it was a lovely sensation to know they were still usable.

After that experience, I was afraid to get back into bed. Instead, I wobbled around the ward looking for familiar faces. This was unsuccessful, so, not wanting to stop walking, I approached a German doctor, who surprised me by speaking almost flawless English but with a heavy German accent. I told him that I wanted to keep busy and keep my legs moving. He called an orderly, who first put me to work sweeping the ward then serving hot soup to those who couldn't get out of bed. I imagined myself as an ugly Florence Nightingale but in reality all I wanted was to keep the life in my legs. The doctor had told me that there were several marks of entry from small pieces of shrapnel in both legs and one foot and that the best thing I could do was to keep them moving, since some nerves could have been severed.

I soon graduated from kitchen work to rolling paper bandages. My big chance finally came when I was summoned to the operating room with three others. If they had issued me with a white gown, who knows, I may have become an instant doctor but the duty turned out to be the holding down of soldiers while they were operated on. We were the anaesthetists, one for each arm and one for each leg. Either there were no anaesthetics or the Germans did not want to waste them on us.

Our first patient had a bullet in his upper leg. The limb was a mixture of angry red, purple and yellow, and as the knife slit him, he screamed bloody murder while pus and blood shot into the air.

His screams changed to vile curses as he called the doctor a 'son-of-a-bitch-of-a-Hun'. This was his most polite epithet. The curses gradually changed to tears and then to laughter as the pressure was relieved, the bullet having popped out with the rest of the gore.

At the end of the day, I was able to have a quiet chat with the doctor. He started by saying, 'What do you think now of our wonderful German army? They stopped the invasion with only one division.' My reply was a sarcastic chuckle as I reminded him that it wasn't an invasion but only a raid in force by about 5,000 men. To back up my point, I handed him a leaflet that had been prepared for the French civilians. As well as I can recall, it read, in French, 'This is only a "coup de main" (raid). Take shelter and do not take any action to jeopardize your safety.' The doctor crumpled it up, claiming that it was only propaganda. His last words to me were, 'Our army knew you were coming and were well prepared. Your security was very bad.'

We spent several days in the hospital at Rouen before we were moved to the railway depot and loaded on to a hospital train headed for Germany. I was still on my feet, so they placed me in charge of a coach holding thirty men. My job was to tend to their every need, their food, their water and at times changing their bandages. The first day was the worst. It seemed that all thirty wanted a drink of water every minute and all of the time. They really couldn't be blamed, since the heat in the coach was suffocating, what with the hot sun beating down on the roof and us forbidden to open any windows. Then one soldier nearly bled to death when his wound opened and the paper bandage, sodden with blood, came apart. I applied pressure to his leg off and on for almost an hour until a German first-aid man arrived on his daily rounds. I was tired and irritable, and this was only the first day.

On the second day, I was approached by a British sailor who somehow had sneaked into our coach from the adjoining one. He claimed that he knew France well and wanted a partner to escape with him. It was tempting, and my mind raced ahead through the first of many fantasies about getting back to fight another day, but I refused for two reasons. First, as much as I hated being at the beck and call of all these men, I just couldn't leave them unattended. Secondly, I wanted to reach our destination, where I believed the Germans would register us and notify our next of kin.

The train stopped frequently on its way through France and Belgium. Apparently the Jerrys wanted to show how many prisoners they had taken. The routine was always the same.

Civilians approached, trying to peer through the windows. They gave the 'V' for victory sign and were promptly chased away.

At one of these stops, I ignored the warning about opening windows or trying to communicate with the population and, after a great deal of banging and lifting, I finally did open a window, shoved my head partly out and tried to converse in my high-school French. It didn't work very well, as all I received in the way of answers were shrugged shoulders and the usual 'V' signs. Behind me, I heard the scream of a German soldier. (They never gave an order; they screamed it. I believe they thought it would terrify us.) I spun around just as the son of a bitch lunged at my gut with his bayonet. I have never moved so fast in my life. I jumped backwards and sucked in my stomach at the same time. The tip of his weapon pierced my tunic but didn't even scratch the skin. We stood frozen, staring at each other in mutual hatred. My mind raced as I tried to figure out my next move, but luckily I didn't have to make one. With an unmistakable gesture, the German ordered me to shut the window. Not being entirely stupid, I did so.

At another stop, a German military photographer boarded the train in order to take propaganda photographs. When he entered our coach, accompanied by a guard, he set up his tripod and trained the camera on me, since I was the only one in our coach who was on his feet. He focused the lens and, just as the flash went off, I thumbed my nose at the camera. Both he and the guard screamed at me and the latter made a run towards me. Instead of a rifle butt, which I expected, he gave me a hard shove, knocking me backwards, and called me a *dumkopf* (blockhead). All I could do was curse silently and pick myself up as they left the coach. I felt sure that this was one photo that would never be published. It was an extremely small victory, but a very satisfying one.

After what seemed to be an eternity, but was actually four long days and four endless nights, we arrived at our destination, the town of Stadtroda. I was glad the journey was over and happy to be relieved of my charges, especially the biggest moaner I have ever met, a British Commando Sergeant with a bad leg wound. He demanded more attention than any of the other soldiers. (I believe it is true that some of the toughest and bravest men usually make the worst patients.)

Much to my surprise, British soldiers in uniform boarded the train. For a moment I thought that we were being rescued, but as it turned out they were members of the British Medical Corps, assigned to the hospital in Stadtroda to work under a British Major

British prisoners, mainly amputees, confined in the hospital
at Stradtroda. The photograph was given to me by the
double amputee in the front row, a remarkable example of
true courage in adversity.

who was a skilled Harley Street surgeon. He in turn was under the German hospital Commandant. We were quickly and efficiently unloaded and transported to the hospital, which was part of Stalag IXC. What amazed me was how the British treated the German guards, with a superior disdain.

There was a large number of other prisoners in the hospital, mainly Serbians and Yugoslavs. They had suffered through a typhus epidemic and we were told that, when they had been brought in, they were like living skeletons, with the fear of starvation in their eyes. This was soon borne out, for when we received our first hot meal in days, which consisted of potatoes and nothing else, most of us ate only a few spoonfuls and put the food aside. The Serbians and Yugoslavs collected all the leftovers in huge pots, sat down in a corner and proceeded to eat the contents like animals. Eventually, we did manage to eat a little better, but only because of the soft diet parcels supplied to us from Britain through the Red Cross. Mostly it was what we called 'pap' food, consisting of powdered milk, dried egg powder, pudding mixtures, etc., which was sent only to hospitals.

Because of the fear of a new typhus outbreak, we were shaved from head to foot, and I mean that literally. No hair escaped the hospital barber and, when my turn came, I almost panicked, not from his shaving my head but from what followed. He held my penis gently between thumb and forefinger and with quick and expert movements of his straight razor quickly denuded me of all pubic hair. I held my breath during the whole operation, expecting any minute for him to cut off my pride and joy and leave me with a high giggle. When he finished there was a loud sigh of relief, not only from me, but from the other prisoners who had jumped out of bed to watch, knowing their turn was coming.

We were fingerprinted and photographed the next day, after supplying our name, rank and serial number. Then we were issued POW dog tags. I became No 43071 and as such, after dark, I stole out of the ward and made my way to the room where I had learned the records were kept. I was an avid collector and just had to see and possess my official prison photo. It was fairly easy to steal but hard as hell to keep, what with the constant searches.

The nights were long in the hospital. It was difficult to sleep while trying to shut out the groans and moans of the wounded. The next bed to mine was occupied by who else but the chief moaner from the train journey. We never spoke; we only glared at each other with mutual dislike. On my other side was a very badly

Name:	Vorname:	Nummer:
Prouse	Arthur, Robert	43071
29.8.42. Kdo 1170 Rü.Lg. Stadtroda	(AE. 7.8.42.)	
2.11.42. Kdo 865	Molsdorf	K 865. 4.11.42.
11.11.42. Kdo 1049	Niederorschel / Eichsfeld K.865. 18.11.42.	
Am 27.4.43 geflohen	wiedervergriffen	
15.5.43 Kdo 865	Molsdorf	(K.865) 17.5.43.
24.5.43 Kdo. 1049	Niederorschel / Eichsfeld	A.E. 27.5.43
am 8.10.43 geflohen	wiedervergriffen	
Kdo: 865	Molsdorf	(Rü.v. 18.6.43. We)
7.9.43	Rü.Lg. Haina	Jan.St 21.9.43
X 15.9.43	865	865/11.40
	Z M.	

Wehrkreisdruckerei IX Kassel

M-Stammlager IX C
Bad Sulza
(Thür.)

The prison record, showing transfers and escapes, was taken from camp
files after liberation. The photograph was stolen the night it was taken
and secreted in the false bottom of a tobacco tin throughout the war.

wounded private, and although he must have been in great pain, he never uttered a whimper. He died within the week as gangrene had set in and could not be curbed, even after amputating his leg.

The worst culprit was another seriously wounded private who slept all day long and commenced his ritual of moaning as soon as lights were out. It was the same cry every night, starting with a prolonged 'Jeeee-sus-Keeeeee-rist', repeated over and over, in long drawn-out syllables. This always started a chorus of shouts from the other patients, ranging from, 'Shut up you bastard' to 'Die you son-of-a-bitch and get it over with.' We finally solved the problem by taking turns waking him during the daytime. As soon as his eyes began to flutter shut, someone would shake him awake.

One of the heroic figures to us was a British soldier, who had been in and out of the hospital for two years. He had been captured at Dunkirk and had since lost both legs. His back had also received bad wounds and was criss-crossed with scars from numerous operations. This brave man never stopped smiling and moving about the ward encouraging the wounded. He travelled along the rails of the beds, which were placed back to back, and could move faster than we could walk. He was only half a man physically, with extremely short stumps, but to us he was seven feet tall.

As a boy I had read in wonder about the soldier whose life was saved by the Bible he carried in his tunic pocket. At the time, I felt that it was an almost impossible miracle. Now I know better, because one of my buddies in the hospital had had a bullet enter his body and stop just short of going through his heart. The main impact was stopped by a wallet full of girls' photos. Another soldier caught a spent bullet square in the middle of his forehead. The hole was puckered and dark and closed, set in about a quarter of an inch inside his skull. He never even had a headache, and the last time I saw him the bullet still hadn't been removed. The airman in the bed next to mine had bailed out of his falling plane. His chute had failed to open and he lived to tell the tale only because he landed in a haystack. This was attested to by the Germans.

One of my best buddies, from the same company as mine, was also in the ward. He had had a bullet removed from his knee and was up and walking to get the leg working properly. We started talking escape and finally agreed to go together as soon as his knee healed. By the time he was ready, my instep had festered and I was scheduled for the operating room. My buddy was itching to go and asked me if I minded if he went alone. My answer was 'No' and that night he took off, leaving his bed stuffed with blankets and clothing to make it appear that he was safely tucked in. (I met him months later and learned that he had boarded a box-car and had ended up near the Czech border—incidentally the wrong direction —and finally had been recaptured.)

The next morning I was picked up early and moved to the operating room. They were well equipped here and gave me a spinal anaesthetic. I sat up and stated that nothing could put me to sleep, and was gently pushed back by the British major who had performed the operation. He said, 'Take it easy, it's all over.' He had removed one large piece of shrapnel from my calf, leaving the smaller pieces alone, stating that they would eventually work their way to the surface. He tried to get the piece in the instep but it eluded him, being too deep in among the many small foot bones.

When I came out of the anaesthetic, my bed was surrounded by patients who could walk. This gathering of an audience around a drugged man's bed was a daily ritual, as every person reacted differently to the anaesthetic: some sang and acted crazy, some sobbed, others fought. This show was one of our few recreations and broke much of the tension. I was peaceful for a while. Then I turned my head and spotted the 'moaner' in the next bed. He had been operated on too, and was also swathed in bandages. With mutual consent we hurled ourselves at each other in hand-to-hand combat. Cheers arose as the beds collapsed and we rolled amongst the sheets and pillows, locked in a deadly embrace and trying desperately to eliminate each other. Guards rushed in and finally pulled us apart, an action roundly booed by the spectators. (Many months later, in the POW camp, we met, both healed and on our feet. It was instant respect for each other and we managed to hit it off very well.)

The remaining days in hospital were passed shooting the breeze, exchanging stories of our experiences on the beach at Dieppe and lining up for our turn in the latrine. There was no question of where it was, as the approach was covered with excreta. The single latrine on our floor, insufficient in size for the large number of patients, was a filthy mess, with the floor, walls and seat completely soiled. The line-up was always so long and the prisoners so ill that most simply couldn't wait. It was a gruesome experience for the fastidious.

We played cards to pass the time and to forget our hunger. We looked forward to mealtimes but they were always disappointing, with potatoes and cabbage being the main fare. We often gave our food away to Russian or Ukrainian patients, since we hadn't previously done without and didn't know the meaning of starvation.

We mainly tried to sleep as much as possible. Sleep was a good healer both for the wounds of our bodies and of our minds, which had been given too great a shock in too short a time. Every so often a visiting German doctor would make his rounds with the resident British POW doctor either to declare men fit to be discharged or to be given more time. The British doctor would always try to buy more time for the men.

We visited other beds on a continuous search for cigarettes, as the only ones available at the time were the French fags, which were strong enough to make you cough and wheeze. Occasionally, Serbian prisoners offered us papers and small sacks of very coarse tobacco kernels, which either pierced the cigarette papers or ended up on the floor.

My period of recuperation lasted until November, when I was discharged from the hospital and shipped to another part of Stalag IXC, on the outskirts of Molsdorf.

3: Niederorschel Work Kommando 1049

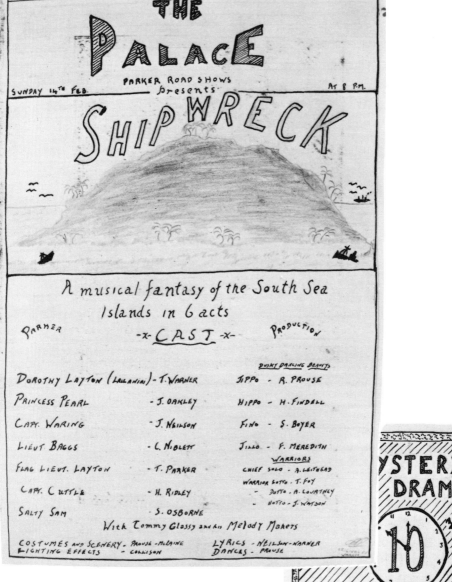

THE PALACE

PARKER ROAD SHOWS
presents

SUNDAY 14TH FEB.   AT 8 P.M.

SHIPWRECK

A musical fantasy of the South Sea
Islands in 6 acts

PARKER   -x- CAST -x-   PRODUCTION

DUSKY DARLING BEAUTY

DOROTHY LAYTON (LALLANINI) - T. WARNER   JIPPO - R. PROUSE

PRINCESS PEARL   - J. OAKLEY   HIPPO - H. FINDELL

CAPT. WARING   - J. NEILSON   FINO - S. BOYER

LIEUT BAGGS   - C. NIBLETT   JILLO - F. MEREDITH
                                          WARRIORS
FLAG LIEUT. LAYTON   - T. PARKER   CHIEF SOLO - A. LEITHEAD

CAPT. CUTTLE   - H. RIDLEY   WARRIOR LOTTO - T. FOY
                                          - DOTTO - A. COURTNEY
SALTY SAM   - S. OSBORNE   - HOTTO - J. WATSON

With Tommy Glassy and his Melody Makers

COSTUMES AND SCENERY - PROUSE - McLAINE   LYRICS - NEILSON - WARNER
LIGHTING EFFECTS   - COLLISON   DANCES - PROUSE

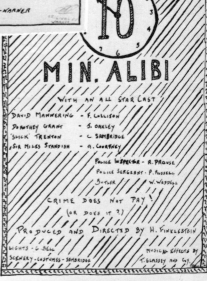

MYSTERY
DRAMA

10 3 ACTS

MIN. ALIBI

WITH AN ALL STAR CAST
DAVID MANNERING - F. COLLISON
DOROTHY GRANT   - S. OAKLEY
'SLICK' TRENTON - L. SAMBRIDGE
SIR MILES STANDISH - A. COURTNEY

POLICE INSPECTOR - R. PROUSE
POLICE SERGEANT - P. RUSSELL
BUTLER   - W. WEDDELL

CRIME DOES NOT PAY!
(OR DOES IT?)

PRODUCED AND DIRECTED BY H. FINKLESTEIN

LIGHTS - G. BELL   MUSICAL EFFECTS BY
SCENERY - COSTUMES - SAMBRIDGE   T. GLASSEY AND CO.

Original plays, recitals, boxing matches and other
'entertainments' were allowed on Saturday nights.
They were abruptly cancelled if any escapes had
been attempted.

CHAPTER 3

Niederorschel Work Kommando 1049

The camp at Molsdorf consisted of a large group of huts surrounded by barbed wire and overlooked by a machine-gun tower equipped with a search light. Guards patrolled the perimeter with police dogs, while other guards intermingled on the inside. It was dusty and dirty in the hot weather and a sea of mud when it rained.

In this camp many of the Canadians were shackled, supposedly in retaliation for Dieppe, where the Germans claimed that German prisoners were found shot dead with their hands tied behind their backs. (Ironically, the cord from Red Cross parcels was used to bind POW wrists until handcuffs became available.) The chains were more of a nuisance than anything else, as within minutes the prisoners had them removed by unlocking them with a key fashioned from the key of a sardine tin. Not having come directly from Dieppe, I was spared the ordeal during my initial brief stay and during my subsequent stints at Molsdorf.

About ten days after my arrival, not having been recognized as an NCO by the German authorities, I was transferred to a work camp, Kommando 1049, in Niederorschel. (Recognition had to come from the military in England. Even though the Germans may have received my papers as well as many others, they could delay the procedure, thus getting as much work out of the unrecognized NCOs as possible. Non-commissioned officers were not supposed to work.)

Outside of a handful of Canadians, the prisoners were all British, most of them having been captured at Dunkirk with the 51st Division. There were corporals, sergeants and sergeant-majors who were still awaiting recognition after two years' imprisonment. While they waited, they were treated as privates, who were compelled to work. The camp was a plywood factory, surrounded by barbed wire, with all sleeping and eating facilities within the factory compound. The entire enclosure was surrounded by more wire, with the usual tower, armed guards and police dogs.

As a Canadian, the Germans took for granted that I must be a lumberjack. They put me to work in the 'yard', piling logs with a cant hook, and taught me how to use a power saw, a tool I had never seen in Canada. At a later date the German Commandant had the new arrivals questioned to see what jobs they would best be suited for. When my turn came, I said that I was a salesman and would be willing to travel. This didn't go down well, as they didn't have much of a sense of humour. I then said I was a writer, figuring that this should get me an easy job, but again there were no openings. Finally, he yelled several names in German. The one that caught my ear and sounded rather cute and easy was the word *tischler*. I didn't know what it meant but I quickly became a carpenter's helper. My boss was a likeable Scottish sergeant named Mac.

The head of the plywood factory had been a prisoner of war in England during the First World War and, having been well treated there, he wanted to reciprocate. Through the Commandant, he advised our confidant man that he would supply wood to line our barracks. A confidant (or confidence) man acted as a liaison between the POWs and the Germans. He would be fluent in German and would be given supplies for his own administrative purposes. It was only through such men that we could 'borrow' ink, etc., for recording our impressions. The building was cold and draughty at the best of times and, since winter had arrived, it was now plain miserable. The confidant man's offer was quickly accepted, and the job was given to the two 'carpenters'. The wood soon arrived, along with a lot of scrap plywood. We shared the plywood among any prisoners who wanted to make a suitcase. (A hollowed out space in the bottom of mine was ideal for hiding my scribblings.)

We soon got to work lining the walls, ceilings and floors of the bunkhouse. We left neat, almost invisible, little trap doors over our own bunks for future use. We also devised a very uneven trap door in the floor, impossible to detect, for a future entrance to a planned tunnel. This tunnel was soon started and the work went quickly. We operated on a twenty-four-hour basis, with men taking turns when they were off their regular factory shift. It was being built for a mass escape, so no pains were spared to ensure its safety. It was to be completely enclosed, with ceilings and walls made with the brand new plywood so generously supplied by the Germans. Not only was it equipped with electricity but also with a small two-way cart which was worked with ropes to haul the dirt out of the tunnel. Later, this dirt was removed to the outside by each man filling his pockets when going on shift to the factory.

One night, when the tunnel was nearing completion, an English prisoner was brought in who claimed to be an escapee from another camp. A Welshman recognized him and later, when we were all seated having our evening soup, he stood up and accused the new arrival of being a spy for the Germans, going from camp to camp to ferret out escape information and then passing it on to the Gestapo. The Welshman claimed that in two other camps in which he had been held, this same prisoner had arrived from a so-called escape then had disappeared within days, with the Gestapo arriving shortly after and going directly to tunnels under construction. The new arrival was warned that he would be watched closely and that, if the Gestapo arrived before our tunnel was finished, he would be severely dealt with.

The Englishman disappeared that night while the camp slept. The Gestapo arrived the next day and went directly to the well-concealed entrance we had built. This was enough evidence for most of us that he indeed was a spy and if the usual German method was used, he was repaid with a certain amount of freedom and better food, with wine and women thrown in. This prisoner was now a marked man and word went out through the grape-vine to be on the lookout for him. I never saw him again but, if he lived through the rest of the prison life, it was assured that he would face a court-martial if and when he returned to England.

As my first Christmas in captivity drew near, the head of the factory put in a request for two artists to hand paint wooden toys made by the workers for their children. We felt that since he had been kind enough to supply the camp with wood, Mac and I should volunteer our services. The following day we were escorted to a workshop where the finished toys were lined up awaiting our artistic endeavours. The German in charge was a cross-eyed imbecile we named 'Boss Eye', who immediately questioned me about Canada. He first stated that it must be wonderful for me to see the trees and flowers in Germany (that is, in the summertime), as he was convinced that these things did not exist in my homeland. He then wondered why I was white skinned, being under the impression that Canadians were either Indian, Eskimo or black. I told him that I had a white mother who had married an Indian chief. His crossed eyes lit up as a new look of respect entered into them.

We didn't last the week as artists. We were fired. It wasn't that we didn't do a good job but that we did it much too well! We painted about two or three dozen dancing dolls. These were the type that were suspended between two sticks so that they danced and jiggled as you squeezed the sticks with your hand. We painted

Left : This 1941 photograph shows British prisoners captured at Dunkirk who were assigned to Work Kommando 1015, the salt mines at Bischofferode. Two of the men were later my room-mates in Mühlhausen.

Below : Group of plywood factory workers at Niederorschel, most of whom were captured at Dunkirk. Some of these men were beaten for the work ultimatum and sent to hard *strafe* in Poland.

WEEKLY

FAT	2.4 oz	MEAT	5.7 oz
POTATOES	7 lb 11.2 oz	SAUERKRAUT	1 lb 5.4 oz
MARGARINE	5.35 oz	CHEESE	2.2 oz
BREAD	5 lb 12.3 oz	JAM	6.25 oz
BARLEY	4.46 oz	SAUSAGE	2 oz
SUGAR	6 oz	CABBAGE OR TURNIPS	2 lb 3 oz
COFFEE (ERSATZ)	0.625 oz	PEAS	3.5 oz
	(approx $\frac{1}{2}$ oz)	MILLET	1.75 oz

DAILY

ONE LOAF BROWN BREAD (1800 GRAM) BETWEEN,

5 MEN FOR HEAVY WORK	NOW THE LOAF IS
6 ,, ,, LIGHT ,,	2000 GRAM BETWEEN
7 ,, ,, NO ,,	9 MEN (SINGLE CUT)

(APPROX—3–4 SLICES PER MAN)

ONE SMALL PORTION MARGARINE

ONE BOWL ($\frac{1}{2}$) OF SOUP (EITHER PEA–POTATO–
CABBAGE–TURNIP–BARLEY–MILLET OR
SAUERKRAUT) FAT IS PUT IN SOUP
(MEAT IS PUT IN SOUP)??
JAM–SUGAR–COFFEE–CHEESE–SAUSAGE–(ISSUED
WEEKLY, AS TOO SMALL FOR DAILY ISSUE)

The above is supplemented by Red Cross parcels—(contents
as shown below)—one parcel per man, per week—until
transport slowed up from bombing—now $\frac{1}{2}$ parcel per man
(if arrive)

The contents of our weekly* parcel:—

Bully beef	—1 Tin	Salt	—1 Pkt
Meat Roll	—1 ,, (SPAM)	Biscuits	—1 ,, (12)
Salmon	—1 ,,	Prunes	—1 Pkt
Sardines	—1 ,,	Raisins	—1 ,,
Jam	—1 ,,	Soap	—1 Bar
Cheese	—$\frac{1}{4}$ lb	Chocolate	—1 ,,
Sugar	—$\frac{1}{2}$,,	The above is contents of a Canadian
Coffee	—$\frac{1}{4}$,, (sometimes tea)	parcel—others vary.
Powdered milk	—1 Tin	*(now a two-weeks issue)

The list of daily rations was a joke, especially the references to meat
and cheese.

about half of them as skeletons and half as little Hitlers, complete with the cropped moustache and a hank of hair drooping over the forehead. 'Boss Eye' took a dim view of our wit, saying that the skeletons would scare the kids and that, if the German officer saw the little Hitlers, he would most likely have us shot.

Our real downfall, however, were the battleships. When we had them all painted, we commenced lettering them with names of German ships which we knew had been sunk by the Allies. We had just finished when the factory foreman came in to see how we were progressing. His eyes lit up at first, as they really looked good, but when he picked one up and examined it closely he said, 'This ship is *kaput*.' Then, as he picked up one after another, he said, '*Allus kaput*.' 'Boss Eye' then showed him the dolls and that was the last straw. He screamed at us and called the guards to escort us back to the camp.

That first Christmas in Germany was a lonely one. It started me thinking too much of loved ones and home. I began to formulate thoughts of escape. We received Christmas crackers from an organization in England and were extremely surprised when 'popping' them to find map sections falling out. Each map section showed various parts of Germany plus adjoining countries, such as Belgium, Holland and France. They were on very thin rice paper and were an invaluable asset for would-be escapees. We silently thanked the powers who had devised this method of delivery, at the same time wondering how it had been missed by German Intelligence.

The maps gave us all feelings of hope and elation (the same feelings we got when hearing some 'good' propaganda, even though it often turned out to be false), and helped overcome some of the recurring feelings of depression, loneliness, anxiety and fear of what the future held. It gave us a lift to know that we were not 'lost' and completely forgotten.

As a matter of fact, our spirits were lifted so high that we became quite bold. Shortly after Christmas a general meeting of prisoners was called to discuss the failure of the Germans to recognize the NCOs. A vote was taken and it was decided to give the German Commandant an ultimatum, demanding our recognition the day after New Year's Day. The idea was to refuse to work if recognition did not come through by then, as we were sure that many of the NCOs' papers were in German hands and were being held back in order to extract as much work as possible from us. The Commandant called a parade, first trying to reason with us and then quickly changing his reasoning to threats. He said that we would lose all privileges such as the Saturday night boxing matches and concerts that had been organized by the prisoners. Then he threatened to cut off our rations and Red Cross parcels. Finally, after each threat had been met with a cheer, he lost his temper and stated that we would all be taken out of camp, one by one, and shot. When this remark was also cheered, he stamped out of the laager in disgust.

On the day of the deadline, all prisoners arose extra early to see what the day would bring. We did not have to wait long. A large number of guards with fixed bayonets stormed in and herded all the prisoners together, jabbing and butting, until we were completely surrounded. Then a high-ranking German officer marched in, followed by a large group of Gestapo. He ordered that those on the shift due at the factory should march out immediately. There were shouts of refusal from the prisoners and then a barked order from the officer. The guards started to beat those in the front rows with their rifle butts. As blood started to flow and men fell, our leader called for a halt and advised the men that they had better move out since it was hopeless for unarmed men to oppose the Germans any further. We obeyed and those on the morning shift left the building with the Germans following closely behind. It wasn't until this shift returned that we learned what had happened. Apparently the men had entered the factory and stood to attention at their machines but refused to operate them. The guards again started to beat them with rifle butts. All finally gave in except for four men, a 'Taffy' (Welshman), two Englishmen and one Scot. Those returning said that every time one of these four was knocked down, he would get back up, stand to attention and shout 'God save the King'. All were finally knocked unconscious and dragged away, and we later learned that for disobeying an order they were sentenced to two years' hard labour in Polish salt mines. The results of the defiance seemed worthless at the time, but a few months later recognition papers started to come through, and eventually all NCOs were moved to non-working camps.

After our act of defiance, the camp settled down to a normal routine. We were up each day at 6:00 a.m., and until 'lights out' at 10:00 p.m. the day was organized around a boring schedule punctuated by mealtimes and welcome cigarette breaks.

The German food was insufficient and tasteless. It consisted of a steady diet of rotting potatoes, cabbage, sauerkraut and black bread. This was the daily fare. Once, we received a type of soup

Above : I represented Canada in the group on the right at the funeral of a British corporal accidentally electrocuted at Niederorschel.

Left : Photos of funerals and gravesites were sent to next-of-kin as propaganda. POW honour guards were issued new uniforms only for the duration of the funeral services.

that was 'blood-red' in colour and had the consistency of blood. I managed two spoonfuls and shuddered as the sticky mess stuck to the inside of my mouth. It was hard to swallow and went down very slowly, leaving a nauseating effect in the throat and stomach. It affected everyone the same way and all prisoners refused to eat it, complaining bitterly of its taste and appearance and swearing that it *was* blood of some type. Fortunately, it was never given to us again.

Once a week each man also received a very small portion of ersatz (substitute or artificial) jam and sugar. With very careful rationing, we were able to make this last a day. The daily coffee was also ersatz, usually made from acorns. Without the Red Cross parcels, we would have gradually starved. These parcels were supposed to arrive once a week but often were not issued. When they did not appear, the Germans would claim that they had been lost in air raids by the Allies but, on several occasions, 'Crazy-legs', the Commandant, was seen eating 'bully-beef' from a British tin. When the parcels did arrive, it was heaven. These and the mail, plus the thought of escape, were the things that kept us going from day to day.

During the winter, the camp leaders usually organized plays, concerts or boxing matches to ease this 'hum-drum' life. The costumes and stage back-drops were extremely 'make-shift' but the ingenuity of some men in preparing them was amazing. I got involved for the fun of it and took the part of a 'police inspector' in one play and a 'dancing girl' in another. The latter was a South Seas skit and I wore a grass skirt (made of shredded paper) and a bra to match. There were four of us 'girls' in the chorus line and we got a lot of good-natured 'cat-calls' from the audience, along with a few lewd suggestions.

The 'girl' we really felt sorry for was a New Zealand native Maori. He was the quietest and most polite man I have ever met. We had to do a lot of cajoling to get him into the play, as he was also extremely shy. It was my job to work out the dance routines and we'd 'split a gut' with laughter every time we practised. On the night of the concert, we had to literally drag our friend onto the stage, where he wriggled and squirmed in embarrassment rather than in the practised routines.

My big moment came not in theatricals, but in the boxing ring. I was approached by the camp's confidant man and invited to fight him in one of the bouts. He was strong looking and well over six feet tall. I took a close look and politely refused, mumbling something about never having fought in the ring. He persisted, saying that I was the only one in the camp anywhere near his size and that the bout was mainly to entertain other prisoners and was not to be taken seriously. He also said that he would take it easy on me. I hoped so, as he was well over 200 pounds to my 170.

Against my better judgement, and mainly from embarrassment, I finally agreed. The rest of the group made me feel real good by stating, 'He'll kill you, but we'll be rooting for you anyway.' I wasn't scared, I was terrified, and died a thousand deaths waiting for the weekend to arrive. I felt like a miniature poodle going against a British bulldog, but I couldn't back out with the 'honour' of Canada at stake, not to mention my own.

All too soon, fight night arrived. When it came to my bout, I climbed into the ring on rubbery legs trying to look nonchalant, which is pretty hard to do when every muscle is trembling. I even tried some pre-fight knee-bends but my legs kept buckling, and my main exercise was in trying to stay on my feet. My other problem was trying to breathe. I had stuffed my mouth with cotton in order to protect my teeth but all it was doing was 'gagging' me. I tried to pull the cotton out but couldn't grasp it with my boxing gloves and gave up the attempt as I heard the death-knell, the starter's bell!

I turned slowly to face my opponent and caught a fleeting glimpse of the 'take it easy' Irishman rushing towards me. He looked like a charging bull and he bared his teeth as he moved in for the kill. I only had a second to wonder why he looked so mad as abject fear left me and self-preservation came to my rescue.

I was fortunately blessed with very long arms and stuck the right one out in a straight line to block his wild charge. I felt like a reprieved man when, along with a lot of dancing and prancing about, the stiff right arm worked and I was able to keep him at bay for the rest of the round.

Between rounds, instead of drawing deep breaths, I wheezed and gulped as I tried to get some air past the cotton. It was hopeless. All I could do was to try and get enough air through my nose. (Once again being blessed with a big one!)

I repeated my strategy through the second round and, when I came out for the third and last round, I found that I had gained some confidence. I now knew that I could keep him at arm's length and at least slow down his mad rushes as he tried to demolish me. I even managed to get in a few pokes of my own, along with many wild swings. He had become infuriated and, by losing his temper, had left a few openings. The final bell was like music to my ears and I was elated, not only to be alive but to be unhurt. They called the match a draw, which made me feel even better.

The following day, 'Irish' was still mad and berated me for my lack of boxing skills. I reminded him about his remark of 'taking it easy'. He replied, 'I tried to, but your stupid right arm stuck straight out and stopped me from getting at you. It also made me mad.' I answered, 'That's a lot of bull. You charged at me from the opening bell.' His quick reply as he stalked away was, 'That's because I wanted a quick "knock-out" to please the crowd.' So much for a 'take it easy' pal!

While these diversions made life bearable, we had our share of tragedy, too. An English prisoner, who in peacetime was an electrician by trade, had been put to work taking care of the factory's and camp's electrical needs as an assistant to the German civilian electrician. Late one afternoon, he was accidently electrocuted. He was carried into the laager to be laid out, awaiting burial at a military funeral. The same afternoon, a Canadian by the name of Cal received news that his Dad had died. He wanted desperately to get home and suddenly seemed to go off his rocker. He tried to scale the barbed wire in daylight and was caught immediately. He was lucky not to have been shot. The Germans, realizing his state of mind, turned him over to the prisoners' care.

His condition did not improve and it was decided to lock him up within the camp for his own protection. We were all sitting in the long dining hall enjoying our evening activity of bridge and poker when we were startled by screams and shouts coming from the courtyard. There was a rush for the windows. The blackouts were removed and the light from the windows lit up a strange scene. Cal, who had stripped naked and had forced his body through the bars on his temporary cell, was screaming and fighting with three or four guards in an effort to escape.

When the light from our windows suddenly appeared, one of the guards, thinking it was a possible attempted break-out, fired his rifle blindly into the men standing at the windows. Fortunately, only one man was hit, falling backwards with a bullet through his shoulder. The commotion gradually subsided and the wounded man was taken to the hospital. Cal was locked up again, but this time wooden planks were nailed over the bars to stop him from making another attempt at getting away. Since Mac and I did not have to leave the building or work any night shifts, we were elected to guard the door of his cell. During the night, we could hear him pacing like a wild animal. He must have been desperate, as he kept trying to break down the door. Then we would hear him trying to force the wall between his room and the one where the dead electrician lay. The next night, it was decided that he would be let out and confined to the large dining hall with Mac and me to keep him company. We thought this would give the other prisoners a chance to sleep, since they had been complaining of the noise of Cal hurling himself against the walls.

From midnight until about two in the morning, it was comparatively quiet. Mac and I played cribbage, while Cal continued his frantic pacing. We tried to settle him down with talk but he wouldn't even answer us. Suddenly he made a mad rush towards the padlocked half door that hung over the counter leading into the kitchen. He disappeared through the shattered wood and, by the time we could get through the opening, he had broken down the door separating the kitchen and the guards' sleeping quarters. When we finally reached him, Cal was trying to wrest the rifle from the guard on duty, who had entered the sleeping quarters on hearing the commotion. The other guards, who had been rudely awakened, were sitting up in their bunks; some of them were actually screaming in fear. It took our combined strength to subdue him. Finally he had to be hand-cuffed and bound to stop him from injuring himself or being shot in any more mad escape attempts. The following morning he was taken to the hospital for examination, then put under close confinement. Months later, he was quiet and subdued and very much improved, his grief having faded to some extent. The only signs of his problem were an outward show of defiance to the Germans and a disregard for danger, but these were good signs for a POW.

As the camp routine became established, my mind returned to thoughts of escape. With this intention, I asked for a move from my cushy inside job back outside to log handling. This was quickly accomplished, as there was a line-up of men waiting to trade places with me. While working with the outside gangs, one had to get permission to go to the latrine. This was the usual multi-seat type with a roof and sides but nothing to aid one's privacy. It was open to the elements and cold as hell. Still, it was a kind of haven, where you could sneak a smoke and get away from the job and the ever-watchful eye of the guard. Naturally, there was a separate guard just to watch the latrine and roust you out if you took too long. It was always overcrowded.

After watching and listening, I finally learned how to beat the system. I'd go in one end, push through the crowd and come out the other side, which was partially hidden by sheds and the back of the plant's boiler room. The door that led into the plant was not locked during the daytime and I found that, by making my way through the boiler room and into the main plant, I could dodge the civilian bosses and make my way to the office building latrines. (This building was practically empty, for reasons unknown.) The latrines, or I should say washrooms, were clean and warm but not as private as I thought. I soon learned that a few other prisoners had discovered them. I was in one of the cubicles, on one of my daily visits, when the outside door opened. I could hear two English prisoners approach. I quickly pulled my feet up and stayed put, not wanting to let them, or anyone else, know of my where-abouts. (In prison you acquire an air of suspicion and secrecy when even thinking of escape.)

The two men were discussing some box-cars being loaded with lumber on a nearby rail siding. Their idea was to volunteer for the loading gang, make a hiding place within the wood and eventually wind up in Spain. When I heard this, I felt a little disappointed, as the idea had also occurred to me, but it was an unwritten law that when you became aware that others were attempting the same plan you would drop your idea immediately so as not to jeopardize their escape.

As I emerged from the cubicle, the door on the other side opened and another prisoner stepped out. As we came face to face, he grinned. He had also been eavesdropping and, when we began talking and exchanging ideas, I learned that he had had the same idea. The meeting marked the beginning of a new friendship that would eventually lead to two escapes.

The waiting and waiting for the war to end was hard on men's spirits. Christmas celebrations, meagre as they were, brightened our lives but intensified the longing for home.

KRIEGSGEFANGENENPOST

AIR MAIL
PAR AVION

Escapa

CPL PROUSE. A.R. 43071

LAGER. BEZEICHNUNG. 865

M. STAMMLAGER IXC Iowa

ARBEITS. KOMMANDO NR 1049

DEUTSCHLAND

ALLEMAGNE. 865

Mouvement Pétain
DU STALAG III A

Le Camarade **Abadie Jean**

Matricule No **53655** a adhéré au MOUVEMENT PÉTAIN

du Stalag III A, sous le No **12132**, et déclare faire sienne la

formule portée au verso.

L'ADHÉRENT :   POUR LE COMITÉ :

It was tempting to try and crash the front gate at Mühlhausen. One POW sauntered out quite casually one day, only to be returned and severely beaten.

Left, above : The first of my letters to be marked 'escaped' (April, 1943).

Left, below : The membership in the *Mouvement Pétain* was received in a trade with a French POW.

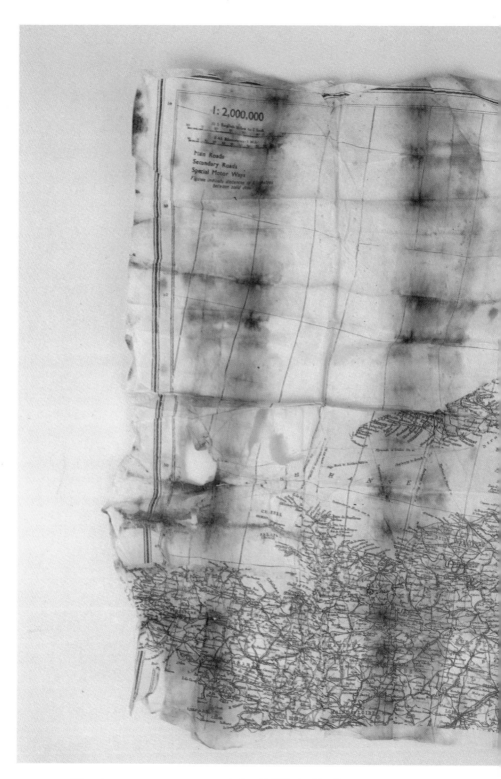

The rice paper map was smuggled to POWs inside Christmas crackers. I hid mine

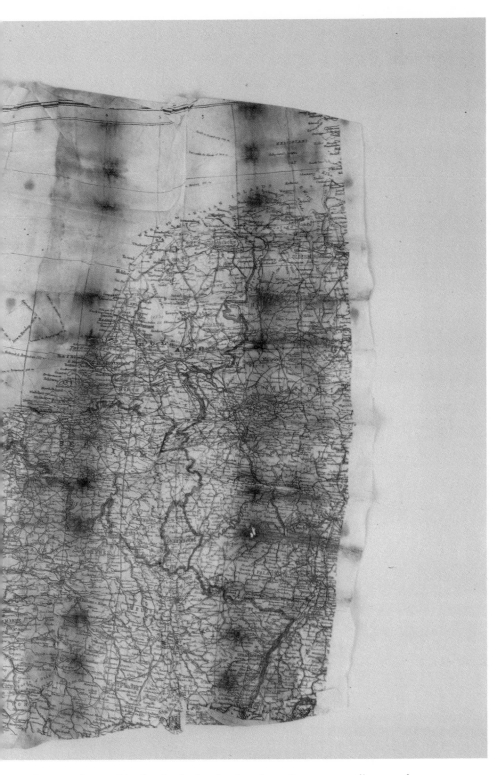

between layers of leather in the insole of my boot. It was never discovered.

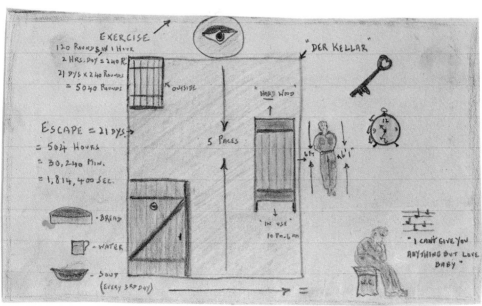

Above: When serving time in solitary, POWs had only about an hour a day to continuously circle the small exercise yard.
Below: The smallest detail becomes very important to a prisoner left alone for twenty-one days.

Rhyming nicknames were popular. Mine was usually some variation on Mickey or Minnie Mouse.

Mühlhausen, the 'castle on the hill', was such a prominent landmark that Allied air forces used it to guide them on their bombing runs over German cities.

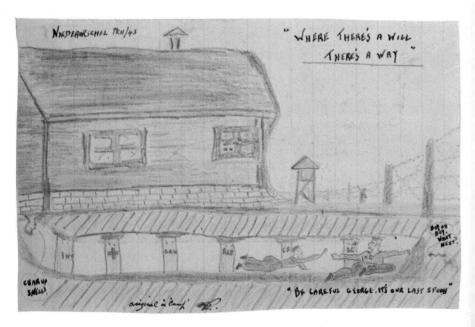

Camps became criss-crossed with tunnels. Molsdorf was so seriously undermined, the POWs had to be moved.

4: The Escape of
Janek Mrachek

Pte. Sinclair - Canada - Killed whilst attempting escape

Pte. Ingram - Scotland -   "   "   "   "

   "   Cruikshank - England -   "   "   "   "

   "   Radwell -   "   "   "   "   "

   "   Collie   -   "   "   "   "   "

   "   Dawson   -   "   "   "   "

Cpl. Ormerod -   "   -   "   during bid for freedom (S.)

   "   Collison -   "   -   "   accidently at work (electrocuted)

Pte. Sneddon - Scotland -   "   "   "   Salt mine (fell in Vat)

   "   Watts   - England -   "   "   in Salt mine cave in

   "   Abaan   -   "   -   "   after assault on guard

   "   Drury   -   "   -   "   Died from injuries in Salt mine cave in

   "   Cowan   - Scotland -   "   under operation

   "   Gatecker - Canada -   "   "   from wounds

(and all other comrades killed whilst attempting escape, whilst
working and from R.A.F. raids over Germany.)

Remember - all P.O.W. who have suffered punishment + imprisonment
       for resisting this life - by escape - refusal of work + sabotage etc.
(a few of the many are):-   Sgt. Jock McPhail. Sgt. Peter Russell. Cpl. Doc. Williams.
           Cpl. Taffy Williams - they refused to work - were beaten
           with rifle butts + sentenced to one + two years in Poland.
Cpl. Jixcock. Pte. McDonald - Pte. King - Cpl. Dave McKenzie. Pte. Bill King - they struck
their captors + were sentenced to time in Poland.
            Pte. Ginger King - Four year prison. who served two
years hard servitude for "sabotage" - + came out smiling!

CHAPTER 4

The Escape of Janek Mrachek

My cubicle partner was Tommy Glassey, a sergeant in the 51st Division, Imperial Forces. He was not tall in stature, but I was to learn that he was very 'tall' in coolness and courage. He was a good looking Scot with a quiet and friendly nature. When we weren't discussing escape, he would wander from room to room strumming on his banjo. One of his friends, a private by the name of Pat, asked if he could join our escape attempt and was readily accepted. Pat, I believe, was from Glasgow, tall, rangy and very thin. Like Tommy and me, he had a restless spirit that dreamed of escape and adventure and he longed to get back into action.

Apart from periodic meetings and discussions on our plans, we didn't fraternize too much and all talk was very secretive. Towards the middle of April, we started to plan our escape in detail. What made the plan feasible was that Tommy had learned to speak fluent German in the two years since his capture at Dunkirk. Our goal was to reach France, obtain sanctuary in a church and eventually contact the 'underground' for assistance. Tommy was to get the forged travel papers, Pat the money and myself the clothing.

The only typewriter in the camp was in Paddy's office, our confidant man with the Jerrys. It was arranged that Paddy would be absent one night and Tommy broke into his office. He typed up our travel papers, seven for each of us. We planned to take seven short train hops rather than one long trip where our papers would be examined more closely. The names were inserted as Czech *arbeiters* or workers, as some of them were allowed to travel to different cities as workers in war factories. My name was 'Janek Mrachek'.

The next step was to have the papers officially stamped with the travel dates and the German swastika and eagle. This was accomplished by a Canadian who was an expert at carving wood. He carved the stamp out of a potato and, after it was dipped in ink, also stolen from Paddy's office, and applied to the papers, they really did look official.

For the clothing, we traded with longtime prisoners who had managed to scrounge an extra pair of army pants. These were dyed a sickly reddish-brown by using red cabbage and the lead from indelible pencils. Anything we could scrounge that was brown or red was tossed into the large pot stolen from the kitchen. Each night Tommy would stir the stinking brew on our makeshift barracks' stove. The smell was unbearable and was almost our undoing, as the Germans soon were questioning us on its origin. Fortunately they accepted our excuse that the daily ration of cabbage was rotten and had stunk up the whole camp.

Next we needed civilian jackets and hats and, as this was my job, I traded my outside job in the daytime to another prisoner for his factory night shift. I volunteered to carry the two large metal jugs full of ersatz coffee that the men on the night shift were allowed for their break at midnight. During the break we were permitted to use one end of the civilians' canteen. We'd heat up the coffee and eat our snack of one piece of black unbuttered bread which, with a little salt, wasn't too difficult to get down. With the help of the other prisoners who kept watch, ready to warn me, I would crawl underneath the trestle tables to the dark end of the canteen where the civilians hung their hats and coats.

The first night I was able to steal two jackets, which I stuffed into the now empty coffee jugs. When the shift was over at 5:00 a.m., I had no trouble walking past the guards and smuggling the jackets into the camp where they were quickly hidden in the niches I had prepared while doing my stint as carpenter. That same day, we were rousted out of bed by a Gestapo search-party, most likely alerted by the civilians whose jackets were missing. They went away empty-handed, but we were tired as hell that night when reporting for night shift, after having our day's sleep disturbed.

Because of the Gestapo visit and search, I thought it best to lay low. Consequently, during the next few nights, I didn't risk taking any more clothing, particularly since the civilians in the canteen were eyeing us suspiciously. I still carried the jugs and awaited my chance. During this period, I met a civilian in the latrine. He was a retard who swept the floors. I gave him a small piece of chocolate saved from my Red Cross parcel. I then offered him a French cigarette and promised to give him a full pack of Canadian cigarettes when I received my next parcel from home. In exchange, I first asked for bread and later for German money. I began to like this character, even though he was quite simple. As near as I could learn with my limited German, his name was Henry and he had been a cavalry man in the First World War. He claimed that he had been shot from his horse and had landed head first on a rock. This I believed, if nothing else!

Sgt Tommy Glassey, my escape buddy on two attempts, was also the leader of The Melody Makers, the band that supplied music for camp plays and dances.

Over a period of 'dealing' with Henry, I managed to get the required money and, having mentioned a hat to him in one of our discussions, he also proudly handed me a peaked cap of the type worn by many Germans. Later that night I tried it on. By splitting the back with a razor blade, I was able to make it fit me. I was extremely pleased with the German badge pinned on the front but Tommy soon wised me up by telling me that it was a Hitler Youth badge. It was fortunate that he had recognized it, for if I had left it on during escape I would have been quickly singled out and caught.

It was now time for a try at getting another jacket to fit me. The first two fitted Tommy and Pat, not perfectly but they were passable. The third jacket and two more hats would complete our wardrobe. I carried the usual two jugs of coffee when going on night shift and, on the midnight break, while the other prisoners kept their eye on the civilians and guards, I again crawled under the tables and worked my way to the coat rack. My goal was not only to acquire a jacket, but one that would fit me. Most of these jokers were small, with only the foreman coming close to my build. Time was limited and I felt a cold sweat coming over me as I struggled into one jacket after another. Finally I found one that seemed to be tailor-made for me. It was a heavy tweed and I had one hell of a job trying to stuff it into one of the jugs. I got most of it in by forcing it with my foot, and the rest went in easily with an extra kick that caused a sound like a breaking stick. Then I grabbed two hats at random and shoved them into the other jug. I was just in the nick of time, as the break was over and I could hear the shuffle of feet starting to move out. Scrambling under the tables, I watched the feet of the prisoners leaving first and came up amongst them with an enormous feeling of relief.

Once again, we got back to camp without any problems and, as soon as the guards left, I examined my loot. All the garments fitted us perfectly. The only problem was that the identification in the wallet found in the side pocket of the jacket belonged to the foreman, a Jerry by the name of Ratzman. He was a miserable son-of-a-bitch who wore thick-lensed glasses and always seemed to be peering at you. He had absolutely no sense of humour and was constantly losing his temper when we wouldn't work. He usually resorted to calling a guard over, who would give us a few prods with a rifle butt. We fondly named him 'Rat Face', and he and 'Crazy-legs', the Commandant, ran neck and neck in our esteem.

After discovering the owner and learning that the snap I had heard while stealing the coat was caused by the foreman's pipe breaking, I made sure that the coat and hats were well hidden and hoped for the best. We had just crawled into our bunks when the Gestapo charged in and hauled us out of our flea pits for the usual search procedure. The first step was to rip our palliasses apart and throw the straw all over the place. Then they tore a few boards off the floor and ceiling and generally made a bloody mess of the barracks and a nuisance of themselves. The only ones who were really disturbed were the fleas, and I happily noticed some of the guards beginning to scratch. The Gestapo finally left empty handed, overlooking the most obvious hiding place, the unlit wood stoves. Later, feeling quite satisfied, we retired for a well earned sleep.

During the next few days, after trying on our borrowed and dyed clothing, we commenced smuggling our loot out piece by piece, once again using the coffee jugs. After being herded into the factory by the guards, we would take turns when going to the latrine to slip out through a window and bury a piece of the clothing in a nearby ditch. The last items to go out were our passes, money and escape rations. The latter consisted of food we had saved from our Red Cross parcels such as raisins, small pieces of broken chocolate and hard biscuits.

Our next move was to exchange places with three other prisoners who had agreed to take our night shift in return for their day shift. Everything now had been done, except to choose the day of escape. By mutual agreement, we chose April 27.

On the morning of our attempt, we lined up at 5:30 a.m. with the rest of the day shift and moved out of the laager into the semi-dark yard. On the way to the factory, the three of us dropped into the open ditch and lay quietly as the other prisoners and guards shuffled past. We quickly dug up our escape gear, scrambled out of the ditch and hid behind the boiler house. Here, we slit our army trousers with razor blades, to save removing our boots, and then climbed into our civilian clothes. We then headed for the main gate where we hid behind a pile of lumber awaiting the arrival of the night shift civilians who would soon leave the camp and head for the nearby village.

This was the crucial moment, as we planned to leave the camp openly, intermingled with the civilian German workers. The one thing that could go wrong was that our absence would be noticed in the factory before we could get through the gate. We knew that when the day shift arrived, the men lined up, were counted and

PRISONER

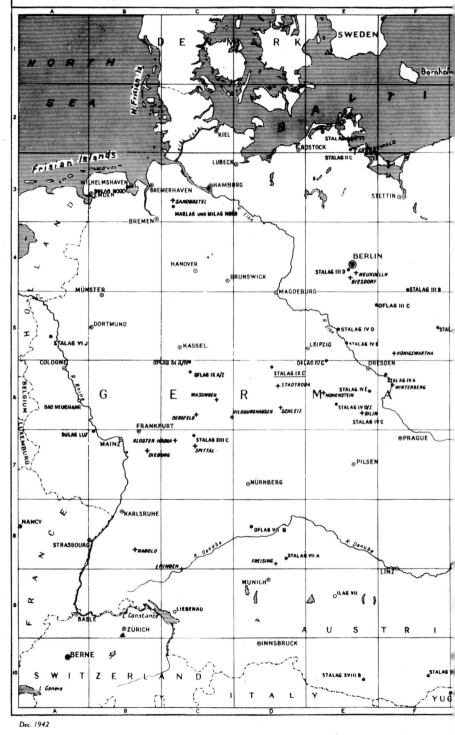

Dec. 1942

The Red Cross supplied maps to wives and relatives in Canada, but

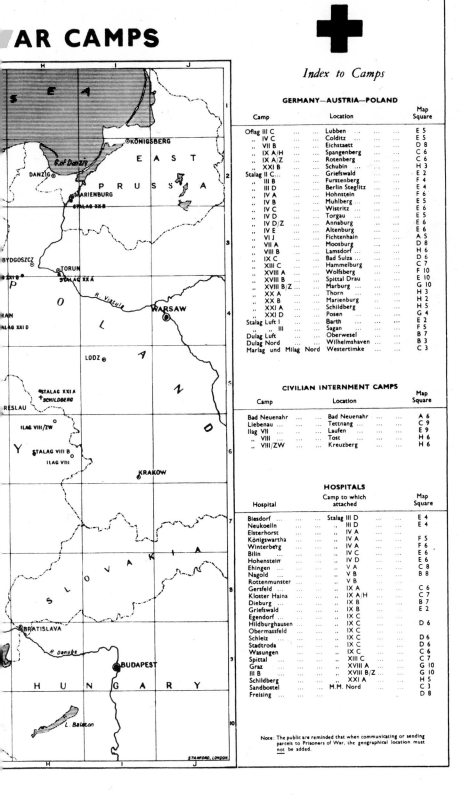

AR CAMPS

Index to Camps

GERMANY—AUSTRIA—POLAND

Camp		Location		Map Square
Oflag III C	... ...	Lubben	... ...	E 5
,, IV C	... ...	Colditz	... ...	E 5
,, VII B	... ...	Eichstaett	... ...	D 8
,, IX A/H	... ...	Spangenberg	... ...	C 6
,, IX A/Z	... ...	Rotenberg	... ...	C 6
,, XXI B	... ...	Schubin	... ...	H 3
Stalag II C	... ...	Griefswald	... ...	E 2
,, III B	... ...	Furstenberg	... ...	F 4
,, III D	... ...	Berlin Steglitz	... ...	E 4
,, IV A	... ...	Hohnstein	... ...	F 6
,, IV B	... ...	Muhlberg	... ...	E 5
,, IV C	... ...	Wistritz	... ...	E 6
,, IV D	... ...	Torgau	... ...	E 5
,, IV D/Z	... ...	Annaburg	... ...	E 6
,, IV E	... ...	Altenburg	... ...	E 6
,, VI J	... ...	Fichtenhain	... ...	A 5
,, VII A	... ...	Moosburg	... ...	D 8
,, VIII B	... ...	Lamsdorf	... ...	H 6
,, IX C	... ...	Bad Sulza	... ...	D 6
,, XIII C	... ...	Hammelburg	... ...	C 7
,, XVIII A	... ...	Wolfsberg	... ...	F 10
,, XVIII B	... ...	Spittal Drau	... ...	E 10
,, XVIII B/Z	... ...	Marburg	... ...	G 10
,, XX A	... ...	Thorn	... ...	H 3
,, XX B	... ...	Marienburg	... ...	H 2
,, XXI A	... ...	Schildberg	... ...	H 5
,, XXI D	... ...	Posen	... ...	G 4
Stalag Luft I	... ...	Barth	... ...	E 2
,, ,, III	... ...	Sagan	... ...	F 5
Dulag Luft	... ...	Oberwesel	... ...	B 7
Dulag Nord	... ...	Wilhelmshaven	... ...	B 3
Marlag und Milag Nord		Westertimke	... ...	C 3

CIVILIAN INTERNMENT CAMPS

Camp		Location		Map Square
Bad Neuenahr	... ...	Bad Neuenahr	... ...	A 6
Liebenau	... ...	Tettnang	... ...	C 9
Ilag VII	... ...	Laufen	... ...	E 9
,, VIII	... ...	Tost	... ...	H 6
,, VIII/ZW	... ...	Kreuzberg	... ...	H 6

HOSPITALS

Hospital		Camp to which attached		Map Square
Biesdorf	... ...	Stalag III D	... ...	E 4
Neukoelln	... ...	,, III D	... ...	E 4
Elsterhorst	... ...	,, IV A	... ...	
Königswartha	... ...	,, IV A	... ...	F 5
Winterberg	... ...	,, IV A	... ...	F 6
Bilin	... ...	,, IV C	... ...	E 6
Hohenstein	... ...	,, IV D	... ...	E 6
Ehingen	... ...	,, V A	... ...	C 8
Nagold	... ...	,, V B	... ...	B 8
Rottenmunster	... ...	,, V B	... ...	
Gersfeld	... ...	,, IX A	... ...	C 6
Kloster Haina	... ...	,, IX A/H	... ...	C 7
Dieburg	... ...	,, IX B	... ...	B 7
Griefswald	... ...	,, IX B	... ...	E 2
Egendorf	... ...	,, IX C	... ...	
Hildburghausen	... ...	,, IX C	... ...	D 6
Obermassfeld	... ...	,, IX C	... ...	
Schleiz	... ...	,, IX C	... ...	D 6
Stadtroda	... ...	,, IX C	... ...	D 6
Wasungen	... ...	,, IX C	... ...	C 6
Spittal	... ...	,, XIII C	... ...	C 7
Graz	... ...	,, XVIII A	... ...	G 10
III B	... ...	,, XVIII B/Z	... ...	G 10
Schildberg	... ...	,, XXI A	... ...	H 5
Sandbostel	... ...	M.M. Nord	... ...	C 3
Freising	... ...			D 8

Note: The public are reminded that when communicating or sending parcels to Prisoners of War, the geographical location must not be added.

STAMFORD, LONDON.

warned them not to add place names to parcels sent to the camps.

answered a roll call. The other prisoners were going to do their best to confuse the count by moving around frequently and answering when our names were called.

The wait seemed endless before the workers appeared but it was actually only a few minutes. They were in a large, scattered group and were headed for the main gates. We joined them unnoticed, as we had hoped, counting on their weariness and disinterest in each other at that time of the morning. The guards opened the gates and we trooped through with a feeling of exhilaration. This quickly evaporated when we found ourselves facing the incoming shift. Most of the workers had their heads down and didn't worry us, but in their lead was none other than 'Rat Face', now in charge of the day shift.

We could not avoid a face to face confrontation without arousing suspicion, and although he ignored my two partners, he peered intently at me through his thick lenses. I didn't know whether he had spotted his jacket or whether my large and recognizable nose had caught his attention. All I could do was return his stare and pray for the best.

For a split second, I thought of distracting him by handing him the two pieces of broken pipe which were still in the pocket but, instead, I yelled 'Heil Hitler' and threw my arm up in the German salute. He quickly returned the salute but, as I passed him, he stopped dead in his tracks. I could feel his eyes boring into the back of my head and I had the impulse to run fast and far away. Suddenly, the tension was broken as the sirens began to wail, announcing our escape. This gave wings to our feet. We took off, knocking civilians right and left as we hustled through their midst.

We jumped a fence, left the road to take to the fields and finally made it to scrub brush without hearing a shot fired. Quickly, we forded a small stream and then climbed a steep railway embankment before stopping to catch our breath and look back. The sirens were still screaming and we could see about fifteen or twenty guards running through the fields toward the embankment. As near as we could tell, about three or four of them were being jerked forward by police dogs. We took off again, sliding and slipping down the far side of the embankment. After running a short way through an open field, we entered the dense evergreen forest which had been our immediate destination. For the next fifteen minutes we never stopped, proceeding deeper and deeper into the wood at as fast a pace as we could manage. Finally, we dropped in sheer exhaustion and tried to catch our breath. Then we slowly crawled under the lowest and thickest branches we could find, each man selecting his own tree for concealment.

It was not too long before we heard the barking of the dogs. Fortunately they weren't bloodhounds and were only trained to drop a man on sight. Next we heard intermittent rifle shots as the guards tried to flush us out of hiding. I thought for a moment that they had spotted one of the others but lay motionless anyway. Then I realized that this was their method of trying to have us break cover. It seemed like a lifetime laying there. I must have died a thousand deaths as my imagination worked overtime. All of a sudden I heard the approach of the guards and dogs. I ventured a peek and could see jack boots and dogs' paws no more than six feet from me. I held my breath and tried desperately to control the tremor that ran through my body, feeling certain that the guard would hear the furious pounding of my heart. Finally, the feet moved off, gradually receding into the distance. Others approached and passed but no one else came that close.

It had been 6:00 a.m. when we first walked through the gates and we later estimated that it had taken us about an hour to reach our place of concealment. It wasn't until around two in the afternoon that we slowly came out of our hiding place, looking at each other and grinning with relief and the first feeling of freedom. We didn't venture out of the woods until about 10:00 p.m. We then slowly made our way to the railway embankment, which we climbed, and then sat on the tracks looking down at the lights in the windows of our former prison. We had a light snack and waited for the freight train that usually passed the camp nightly. It finally came but was faster than we had previously estimated, making it impossible to board. There was nothing left to do but walk the tracks to the nearest freight yards in Leinfelde. On our arrival, we boarded a box-car, laying flat on the roof's cat-walk and hanging on for dear life as the train slowly shunted off into the darkness.

It was a long night and the rushing wind felt unusually cold for April. Our fingers were numb and stiff from the prolonged grip, which we were afraid to loosen. When dawn finally broke and the train began to slow, we clambered down the side ladders and jumped, tumbling head over heels down the embankment.

We found the nearest road. While walking through the first village, we felt sure that the natives would come rushing out at any moment as our army boots clumped over the cobblestones, sounding to us like a cavalry charge. Finally we arrived on the outskirts of

Heligonstadt and located a deserted shack, where we slept for a few hours. Upon awakening, we shaved and tried to make ourselves look presentable for the walk to Kassel, our next destination.

When we arrived in Kassel, which was a fairly large city, we located the station and Tommy purchased the tickets for the first leg of our planned journey. This was uneventful and it didn't seem too long before we left the train at Warburg, where we learned that there was no connection until the following morning. We sat around the station trying to appear nonchalant and spent a lot of time in the toilets, where we nibbled on our rations. We soon became a little bolder and bought a few beers. These made us drowsy and we put our heads on the table and soon passed into the land of no worries, sleeping like three babies.

In the morning, we awakened with a start and had one hell of a surprise. The large round table was covered with the arms and heads of other sleeping figures, all German soldiers, also awaiting the morning train. We eased our way out and took refuge in the toilets, where, after washing and shaving, we assumed a new courage.

My buddies left me standing on the platform while they went in to the station to buy the tickets. The train arrived and passengers hurriedly boarded. As it slowly started to move out, I panicked. I couldn't see Tommy or Pat anywhere. I approached a platform attendant and, in the world's worst German, asked if this was the train for Warburg. (I should have said Arnsberg, our next stopover.) The attendant eyed me suspiciously and told me to wait a minute. He walked into the station taking frequent backward glances. This was enough for me and I jumped on the moving train, feeling very much alone.

Walking from one car to another, I spotted Tommy and Pat sitting together and, with a rush of relief, dropped down in the only vacant seat, beside a German soldier. I found out later that, after purchasing the tickets and hearing the approaching train, they had rushed to the platform through another door, couldn't find me and finally had boarded the train in desperation.

The soldier beside me was very voluble and talked my head off all the way to Arnsburg. All I could do was listen to the intonation of his voice and watch his head as it moved up and down or sideways, giving me the clue to say *Ja* or *Nein*. He was still talking when I left the train at Arnsberg. As we walked along the platform towards the station, a woman with a very motherly face brushed against me and said, '*Aufpassen*' (be careful). She must have been wise to us and may have heard us whispering in English. We'll never know but I mentally thanked her for her motherly concern.

We entered the station and, while Tommy went to buy the tickets, Pat and I entered the ever present beer room and ordered three beers. When Tommy returned, he told us that the station-master had closely inspected the papers and, after some question-ing, had finally accepted them and sold him the train tickets. But we also learned that there was to be a three-hour wait between trains. We had anticipated some brief stopovers, as we had pur-posely planned short hops of 50 to 75 kilometres to avoid too close a scrutiny of our forged passes, but we had not expected such long waits. For a while we had the beer parlour to ourselves and munched on our rations and sipped our beer.

The relaxation did not last long, however, as a large group of German officers trooped in. We felt uncomfortable every time one of them looked at us, so we casually got up and left the parlour and station. We decided to do a little sightseeing to waste time but, just as we began to feel a little more secure, we saw a large group of officers headed towards us. Cowardice being the better part of valour, we ducked into a side street which turned out to be a dead-end with nothing but a steep grassy hill to climb at the far end. Not wanting to retrace our steps, we climbed this hill, which gradually assumed the proportions of a mountain. After much puffing and blowing, we reached the top, where we were surprised to find the ruins of a castle.

As we approached, an apparition in the shape of a very old man seemed to emerge from the ground. Actually, he was coming up a steep flight of stone stairs from one of the lower dungeons. We hesitated until he broke out in a toothless grin of welcome. We soon discovered that he was one of the peacetime caretakers of this tourist attraction called Arnsberg Castle, and was no doubt very pleased to see and hear someone, most likely having been partly forgotten since the onset of hostilities. He kindly gave us the grand tour and explained that Napoleon had been halted here during a French invasion years ago. He made us some ersatz coffee and gave us each two slices of bread, never asking who we were or what we were doing there, nor commenting on Tommy's quiet translation of the commentary. He was simply happy to have someone to talk to.

He gave us hot water to wash and shave with and, when it was time to leave, a part of us hated to go. We knew train time was fast approaching, however, as the hours had sped by during this pleasant interlude. We made our way down the mountain and back to the station just in time to board the train for Hagen.

There were no more unnerving events or challenges in the next three hops and stop-overs to Hagen, Düsseldorf and finally München Gladbach. We could see that all three had received their share of bombs. In the latter city, we discussed whether we should await nightfall and walk to the nearest border village, crossing the border under cover of darkness, according to our original plan, or whether we should take a small local train to the border town of Dalheim and save the walk. At this stage, having had no serious problems or challenges we became a bit cocky and decided to take the train and head for the border in daylight.

We bought our tickets, boarded the train and sat down in long seats running the length of the coach. The rest of the passengers were all workmen returning to their village and evidently all were acquainted with each other. We stood out like sore thumbs, especially in three pairs of purple pants and me with a Hitler Youth hat split up the back to fit my head.

We tried to outstare the locals but there were too many pairs of suspicious eyes watching us. We breathed a sigh of relief as we steamed into the small station and hurried to be the first off. Since the small village was on the border, two huge, elegantly uniformed Gestapo, complete with jack boots and arm bands, were checking the passengers as they entered and exited the station. Being first off the train, we had our papers checked before the other passengers. Surprisingly, they handed them back to us, gave us the 'Heil Hitler' salute and ushered us out of the station doors. We tried to walk slowly and casually down the road towards the border, cursing ourselves that we had not walked the distance and then waited for darkness.

5:If at First...

To all Prisoners of War!

The escape from prison camps is no longer a sport!

Germany has always kept to the Hague Convention and only punished recaptured prisoners of war with minor disciplinary punishment.

Germany will still maintain these principles of international law.

But England has besides fighting at the front in an honest manner instituted an illegal warfare in non combat zones in the form of gangster commandos, terror bandits and sabotage troops even up to the frontiers of Germany.

They say in a captured secret and confidential English military pamphlet,

THE HANDBOOK
OF MODERN IRREGULAR
WARFARE:

". . . the days when we could practise the rules of sportsmanship are over. For the time being, every soldier must be a potential gangster and must be prepared to adopt their methods whenever necessary."

"The sphere of operations should always include the enemy's own country, any occupied territory, and in certain circumstances, such neutral countries as he is using as a source of supply."

England has with these instructions opened up a non military form of gangster war!

Germany is determined to safeguard her homeland, and especially her war industry and provisional centres for the fighting fronts. Therefore it has become necessary to create strictly forbidden zones, called death zones, in which all unauthorised trespassers will be immediately shot on sight.

Escaping prisoners of war, entering such death zones, will certainly lose their lives. They are therefore in constant danger of being mistaken for enemy agents or sabotage groups.

Urgent warning is given against making future escapes!

X In plain English: Stay in the camp where you will be safe! Breaking out of it is now a damned dangerous act.

The chances of preserving your life are almost nil!

All police and military guards have been given the most strict orders to shoot on sight all suspected persons.

Escaping from prison camps has ceased to be a sport!

(over)

This notice appeared on the camp bulletin board shortly before the end of the war.

CHAPTER 5

If at First...

We ventured a backward glance and could see the two Gestapo surrounded by the locals. They were pointing towards us, evidently explaining their suspicions. We continued to walk slowly until we could hear running feet and the shouted command to halt. We turned and slowly raised our hands above our heads as they approached with drawn guns. They asked to see our papers again and this time took a long scrutinizing look. Finally, one of them laughed and told us that whoever had carved the stamp had made a mistake in putting the Swastika backwards. He then singled me out and, pointing to my nose, laughingly stated that, with a nose like mine, I just had to be an Englishman. I did not appreciate his humour.

We later learned that another mistake we had made was that no Czech workers were allowed so close to the border. I also learned that the small stringed tote bag containing my rations had been half hanging out of my coat lining on the train, the red cross on its side plainly visible.

They drove us to the police station in Heinsberg and threw us into the cells. We were left alone for a while but they returned later in the evening to search and interrogate us. They left again and, on their final return, they brought two of their local girl friends to look at us, explaining that the girls had never seen English prisoners!

On May 1, we were transferred to a military prison in Duren. We were put into a large cell with three Frenchmen and one Belgian. The mattresses were the usual flea-infested straw placed on double-decker wooden bunks, but this time void of any blankets. We hadn't been in the cell five minutes when a face appeared at the outside bars. This in itself was remarkable, as we were on the third floor. It was a young Frenchman who handed us half a cabbage and half a loaf of bread. In exchange he wanted any cash, maps or compasses that we had managed to hide during the first search. He claimed that whatever we gave would be passed along to the underground escape organization. We passed what we had through the bars and the face disappeared.

On May 3, we were again moved, this time to the military HQ for a thorough search and interrogation by trained Gestapo. During the interrogation, we supplied the usual name, rank and serial number and professed ignorance of all other matters. They kept asking us about underground organizations and whether we had been helped in any way by German civilians. Our repeated replies were negative, so they finally passed us on to the search guard.

This was embarrassing. First, each prisoner had to stand in the centre of a white circle and disrobe. The clothes were thrown onto a long table where white-smocked and gloved agents tore out the linings and seams and then pried the soles and heels off our boots. While this was taking place, other agents moved down the line in front of us, searching our ears, noses, eyes and mouths. This was bad enough but when they tried to turn my penis inside out I'd just about had it and said so. I received a whack on the side of the head for my trouble and thereafter kept my mouth shut. The final operation was from the 'rear guard'. We were told to spread our legs and bend over while they probed and eyed our rear ends. Anyone holding this job had to be a little perverted, and I wondered what they had to do to earn promotion!

We were returned to our cells and the next day were transported to Stalag VIG in Arnoldsweiler, a place I will never forget for its inhumanity. As we approached the dirt road fronting the camp, we noticed the heads and shoulders of men working in a long ditch outside the barbed wire. They were dressed in green Russian uniforms and seemed to move very slowly, like zombies. As we watched, some of the heads seemed to disappear as if they were falling. We left the truck, entered the camp through the huge barbed wire gates and went through the usual interrogation and search. We were then handed over to a Belgian interpreter, a soldier prisoner like the rest of the inmates. It was his job to process us before we entered the main part of the camp.

We had to strip and be sprayed, while our clothes went into a delousing chamber. Then we were led into the showers, where we were shocked to see naked human skeletons, so far gone that the force of the showers knocked them off their feet. We looked at this macabre scene unable to say a word. We could only stare in disbelief. As we watched, there was a sudden commotion as the German guards rushed in. They screamed at the Belgian for putting us in the wrong shower room and hurried us to a separate and empty compartment. When the guards left, we showered and dried and then waited for the return of our clothes. Finally, the Belgian returned with them, plus a tin bowl for water or soup and three slices of bread per man, our daily ration.

We questioned him on what we had seen and he told us that the Russians were starving to death. They were not members of the International Red Cross and, therefore, received nothing but the miserable German rations. He claimed that twenty to thirty of them died per day and that they were buried in the ditches they were forced to dig outside the camp. While we spoke to him, we tried to re-enter the other showers to give the Russians our bread. He barred our way, saying, 'It's a waste of good food; they're going to die soon anyway.'

When we left the delousing building, two guards led us to the main enclosure. As we entered, the extremely large crowd of prisoners, a mixture of Belgian, Dutch, French, Serbian and Russian, stood at attention and saluted as we were led to a separate barbed-wire enclosure in the centre of the camp. We could not understand this gesture, but later learned that the British army was well respected and that we had been saluted as representatives. The centre enclosure consisted of a brick building housing three or four prison cells. The windows were iron barred and the building was completely surrounded by a high barbed-wire fence. We were alone, completely isolated from the other prisoners.

The cells contained hardwood bunks without mattresses. We were given one blanket but no food other than the bread issued earlier. This was all we were to receive for the day. All we could do was peer through the bars and watch the endless pacing of the other prisoners. As darkness fell, I lay on my bunk and wondered about the future. My eyes soon closed and I could see once again the pitiful skeletons with their skin stretched taut over their bones. Sunken cheeks and eyes made their heads look too large for their bodies. Their buttocks were non-existent and their bellies were bloated. Only their penises looked natural.

I opened my eyes on hearing a slight scratching sound and looked out of the bars. I could see the end of a large pole being pushed through, with a pack of Froggy fags tied to the end. The wonder of the suffering human still helping his fellow man! We relished the cigarettes and then fell into a fitful sleep. On my part, I dreamt of pleading eyes staring out from hollow faces.

In the morning, we were awakened by the guard, who handed us our daily bread ration and a jug of water and then motioned for us to hold our bowls out. From another steaming jug, he filled our bowls with what looked like hot water, though we were expecting ersatz coffee. When he left, we marvelled that for the first time we had been given hot water to shave with, which, without further ado, was accomplished. We sat and waited for our breakfast coffee to wash down a slice of bread. After an hour or so we became impatient and banged our bowls against the outer bars, finally attracting the attention of a guard. When we told him what we wanted, he laughed and told us that he'd already given us our Chinese tea, which accounted for the lemony odour we had noticed in the hot water. We told him what we had done with it and he almost choked in a fit of laughter.

He turned out to be not a bad joker. He had been wounded in action on the Russian front and proved once again that these types of guards, the veterans, were always the easiest to get along with. We finally bribed him with five of our French cigarettes and he sneaked in a jug of coffee. Even without sugar and milk, the heat gave us a lift.

We were confined here for nine days on bread, water and the odd bowl of thin soup, either potato or cabbage. During this period, we checked over the one map we had left, in order to get our bearings. This map had been hidden in the heel of my boot and miraculously had been missed by the Germans. It had been between two layers of leather (not a false heel) and was stained brown, making it difficult to read. For the time being, I kept it in my sock for easy reference. This turned out to be a lucky move.

On May 13, four guards arrived from our own camp to return us to Stalag IXC. Before leaving, an officer came to our cell with guards and ordered us to remove our boots, pants and jackets. In return, they gave us an assortment of army clothing. My uniform consisted of a French hat, Serbian jacket, green Russian pants and Dutch wooden clogs, a sight even a mother couldn't love. I raised hell about my boots, telling them through an interpreter that, according to the Geneva convention, a soldier was entitled to his uniform and boots. Being in civvies when captured didn't help our cause, as it gave them reason to take our clothing, but I still argued because leather army boots were hard to come by and I just couldn't manage the wooden clogs. I thought the officer was seeing my point, as he appeared to be smiling, but the next thing I knew the guards hit me with their rifle butts and ordered me to move out with the others. Not being stupid, I obeyed, but in a final move to show my defiance and displeasure I kicked off the clogs and walked away in my stockinged feet. I'd show them! (Christ, were my feet sore that night!)

They moved us by truck to Köln and then by train on a pic-turesque journey along the Rhine. As we passed through places like

Bonn, Koblenz and Mainz, all we could see were old castles on the tops of the mountains and vineyards covering the slopes. The guards, who were new to us and were all veterans, pointed out places of interest, such as Beethoven's and Goethe's birthplaces. We finally arrived in Frankfurt am Main, where the Jerry guards, who were quite friendly by now, told us that we would sleep overnight. They said that they were supposed to lock us up in the local jail but, as soldiers themselves, they respected us as such and if we gave them our word of honour not to escape they would lock us in a barracks room and see that we had German sausage, bread and beer. We quickly accepted. We couldn't have gone far in our present get-ups anyway and we relished the thought of sausage and beer.

The guards weren't stupid. They wanted to have a night out on the town and told us they were going looking for girls. They had been on 'around the clock' duty. We said that we had too and that we would go with them but our kind offer was refused. The evening was enjoyable and the sausage and beer were out of this world.

On May 14, we were returned to Molsdorf and created quite a stir as we marched into the camp in our unusual get-ups. Nobody could guess which army we belonged to. Once again we were deloused, interrogated and processed, and were then issued with second-hand army uniforms. Entering the camp proper, we were immediately adopted by different combines and fed to the best of their ability. (A combine consisted of from two to four or more men who shared everything they received or could scrounge.) After eating and receiving an issue of cigarettes from the 'escape fund', we were summoned before the British escape committee, which we supplied with all details of our attempt, such as method, route and encounters, to assist future escapes.

We were then asked if we wished to join a planned mass escape through a tunnel in progress. On our affirmative reply, we were relieved of one of our issue blankets, which would be turned over to the camp tailor to be fashioned into civilian clothing.

Before the tunnel was completed, Tommy and I were transferred back to the 'work kommando' in Niederorschel. This was on May 24, 1943. We were immediately assigned to night duty, where a guard was to keep us under his watch for our complete shift. Our job was to work on a massive wood-drying machine, which never stopped rolling. My job was to feed one end with wet plywood and Tommy's job was to remove the dry wood at the other end about thirty or forty feet away. We switched ends on each

69

Fifty-two men escaped from Molsdorf one night in March, 1943.

Only one managed to reach freedom in Switzerland.

shift, since, on the drying end, our hands soon became filled with tiny splinters which caused infection, making it almost impossible for us to close our hands completely.

Most of the first two nights were spent timing the guard who was assigned to us. We soon knew how long it took him to walk the length of the machine, check the man and then walk back again to repeat the procedure. Most important, we knew exactly how long it took him to reach the centre of the machine, which was his only actual blind spot. Both of us were out of his sight for a few seconds. We were too closely watched, on duty or off duty, to organize clothing, passes, etc., but we were determined to have another go.

Previously, when we had worked on the outside gang, we had noted that trucks arrived daily with loads of logs that were dumped into a huge, below-surface vat filled with hot water for soaking the bark, thus making it easy to remove. Beside the vat was a deep pit that housed the steam pipes to heat the water. It was about ten or twelve feet in depth and was usually kept covered with squared logs about the size of railway ties or sleepers. There was usually a quarter-inch space between the logs, just large enough to insert a bar to pry them loose when it was necessary to check the pipes. We had earmarked this pit then as a possible hiding place and now it figured prominently in our new plan of escape.

On return from one of our night shifts, a few days before we were to put the plan into effect, we were summoned before the Commandant who lectured us on the futility of trying to escape and warned us of the consequences. He told us that the guards had strict orders to shoot to kill on any future break. He then had the nerve to hand us a typewritten bill for the loss of our uniforms on our previous escape, uniforms that were Canadian and British and for which replacements were supplied by the authorities in England. We were supposed to pay for them in German POW marks, our earnings for doing their work. The amount for each uniform was 140 marks, or $42.00. The Commandant received our vote for unmitigated gall.

On June 8, when we reported for night shift, it was cloudy and raining and promised to be a dark and moonless night, excellent for our plans. We worked steadily until five minutes before midnight, just before the guard was changed and at a time when he had slowed his endless pacing and was looking forward to his relief. When he reached the centre of the machine, heading towards my end, Tommy took off and got out through a side door of the factory. When the guard checked me and headed towards the other end, I waited until my count told me he was again at the centre, and then I took off for the far end of the factory, which was empty now that the shift had left for their midnight break. (Tommy and I were the only ones left working at this time, since we were usually taken separately for our break by the new guard at 12:30 a.m.)

I ran in a low crouch, using the machines for cover. Just as I reached the end door, I heard the guard yell out in alarm as he discovered that Tommy was missing. I ducked out fast and reached the pit where Tommy had already pried up one of the covering logs. It was a tight squeeze, but we managed to get in and work the log back over us just as the siren sounded, bringing all the guards on the run.

We eventually heard the heavy thud of boots over our heads and the guttural shouts as they hunted in vain. We had worked our way down between the pipes and were laying on a bed of sawdust at the bottom of the pit, expecting to stay there until the search had died down. We had been in the pit for about an hour when we heard a truck overhead. There was a heavy rumble as its load of logs was dumped into the water-filled vat alongside of us. The truck rumbled off and once again there was silence, broken occasionally by the heavy tread of feet as a guard passed overhead. Suddenly we heard a hissing sound and a clanking in the pipes. It didn't take long for us to figure out that the water was being heated and pumped through the pipes into the vat alongside. It eventually became so hot that we were gasping for air. We removed our clothing as the heat became almost unbearable and our naked and sweating bodies were soon covered in sawdust, which caused a terrible itching sensation.

Unable to stand the heat any longer, we decided to chance it and get the hell out of this steam bath. We dressed, leaving off our tunics, which we used on our hands to grasp the hot pipes. We slowly climbed the pipes and pushed our shoulders against the log cover. At first it wouldn't budge but, with a final heave, we moved it free and wriggled through the opening, gasping for air. We tried to replace the log gently but, as it fell into place, there was a squeak and a slight thud. We flattened ourselves face down and held our breaths as the beam of a flashlight broke the darkness. Raising our heads slightly, we got a shock as, about twenty yards from where we lay, we could see the jack boots of a guard who was playing the beam of his light back and forth across the yard.

The hair on the back of our necks stood straight up in apprehension. We expected to hear a shot or a challenge. We literally froze to the ground but for some unknown reason we went undetected and the guard finally moved off in another direction. We figured out later that the guard was looking for standing or crouched figures and neglected to look on the ground.

We lay prone for about five minutes and then worked our way on our stomachs towards the barbed-wire fences. As we climbed, every groan from the wire sounded like a pistol shot. Our clothing kept snagging on the barbs, and the climb seemed endless as we again used our tunics to protect our hands. We finally made it to the top and down through the coils of wire between the double fences, leaving only the outer fence to scale. We went up this fence fairly quickly and, as we both sat on the top strand, there was a loud 'ping' from the wire. We knew this had been heard from the loud shouts and the sound of running feet coming towards our position.

We needed no further encouragement and literally flew from the top strand of wire, landing in a sprawled heap. The siren blared in a long plaintive wail. We took off into the night and didn't look back until we had put a fair distance between us and our pursuers. When we did pause to get our breath, we could see the search-lights circling the area and hear the shouts of the Germans and the barking of their dogs.

Knowing our route well from the first attempt, we had no trouble finding our way in the darkness and rain. Being night time, we did not hole up but kept going until we reached the freight yards in Leinfelde. We hid near the yards, waiting for a freight train to move out. It wasn't too long before yardmen started to shunt some cars and, keeping these between us and the workmen, we clambered into what appeared to be an open coal car and dropped out of sight. As soon as we hit the inside, we were repulsed by the contents, which seemed to be huge hunks of slippery and soft blubber. (To this day, I haven't figured out what it was.) We scrambled to the side of the car, slipping and falling but making no noise in the gooey mess. Finally we made it back up and worked our way over the cars looking for a hiding place and shelter from the now teeming downpour.

We found our shelter on a flat car loaded with German tanks no doubt headed for the Russian front. Crawling under the tanks, we lay flat. It wasn't very good concealment, but at least we were out of the rain. In nothing flat we fell asleep and were only awakened by the sound of voices that seemed to be right beside us. We ventured a peek and could see the figures of men holding lanterns

Bob Prouse - Molsdorf - 1943

J.C. Arnold
1943

British soldier J.C. Arnold sketched this portrait in Molsdorf.

standing almost opposite from where we lay. We held our breaths, expecting them to sight us at any moment, but they were gabbling away while swinging their lanterns and, if they did see us, they never paid any attention.

My legs were cramped from the cold and I was glad when the train moved out again, enabling me to kick out the cramps. We immediately fell asleep again and didn't awake until dawn, finding the train at a standstill in the marshalling yards in Kassel. We were stiff and shivering with the cold as we climbed from beneath the tanks and rolled off the edge of the flat car into the freight yards. There were dozens of workmen busy with shovels and pickaxes. We wondered why we were being ignored by them and suddenly realized that they were either Polish or Serbian prisoners who didn't want any part of us. They worked outside without guards, as there was nowhere for them to go if they did escape, since their countries were occupied.

We climbed the embankment, spotted a Quonset hut and headed for it with the hope of finding a place to wash, shave and clean up in general. Entering the hut, we were surprised to see rows of bunks and every evidence that they had recently been occupied. We found all the necessary equipment for cleaning up and even had fresh water to drink with our mouthful of escape rations. We were just leaving when we saw a large group of men in the distance running towards the hut. They were dressed in shorts and singlets and were evidently on morning PT. We ducked behind the hut as they approached, realizing that they were Jerry soldiers, back from their morning jog. Sneaking away from the area, we headed for Kassel.

We walked around the town for over three hours, still cold and shivering as the rain continued. We realized that we couldn't get far without civilian clothing and finally entered a guest house (beer parlour) to try and warm up. The place was full of foreign prisoners on their morning work break. We ordered a beer and tried to enter into conversation in the hope that they might get us civilian clothing and other help. We tried English, French and German but I think they got the drift of what we were saying but were too fearful of the Germans to give us any assistance. We couldn't really blame them. They didn't know us from a hole in the ground and we could easily have been agents whose job it was to watch them.

We left shortly after having decided to let ourselves be taken and vowing on the next try to prepare properly and only escape if able to procure civilian clothing. It went against the grain to actually give ourselves up, so we deliberately approached every German officer we spotted and, when passing them, we would raise an arm in the German salute and yell '*Heil* Churchill'. To a man, they would all return the salute with a '*Heil* Hitler'. How dumb could they be? We felt this was a good sign, so we continued through Kassel until we reached the far outskirts, finally leaving the city behind.

It stopped raining and the sun broke from behind the clouds, giving us a new lease on life. We headed for a field, lay down in the long grass and were soon in a deep sleep. We awoke in the afternoon and headed for the rails, hopping aboard a slow moving freight and climbing into a coal car. This was hard and lumpy and not very comfortable but it served its purpose until it started to rain again. We didn't want to get soaked and resume shivering, so we decided to try and get under cover. Climbing from car to car, we noticed the engineer looking back as we rounded a long curve and we weren't sure whether or not he had seen us. We finally climbed down the ladder of a box-car that had a cubicle attached to the end. This was not unlike an outhouse in shape and was used as shelter for a guard if the train was carrying munitions. It turned out to be empty, so we entered the tiny space, where we managed by one sitting on the other's knee.

The train rumbled to a stop after about half an hour and a German civilian climbed up and opened the door. I said, 'Hi there, square head. What's cooking?' He answered in German and I said, '*Ja*,' to whatever he was saying. He closed the door and the train started to move again.

Tommy couldn't control his laughter. When I asked him the reason, he replied, 'Do you know what the Jerry was saying?' I told him that I didn't, so he informed me that the German had asked me if we were the two escaping prisoners. Of course, my answer had been, 'Yes'. Consequently, at the next stop we were greeted by the whole village police force and taken into custody.

The procession through the small town was like something out of a comic opera. At the head of the column was the chief, decked out in his best uniform complete with a spiked hat, something that I had only previously seen in pictures of the Kaiser in the First World War. Behind him strode four armed guards, then Tommy and me, followed by four more guards. Bringing up the rear were the villagers, men, women and children, followed by assorted geese and one goat.

We were thrown in the local jail of this small town called Leibenau. We weren't in the cell ten minutes before a package of

French cigarettes was dangling outside the bars, suspended by a thread from the cell above us. Unfortunately, one of the guards on the street below us saw what was going on. He came in, confiscated the cigarettes and told us we'd get no bread as punishment.

On June 11, we were taken to Obervellmar and turned over to the military authorities. We were again thrown in a cell overnight and the following day returned to Molsdorf.

6: The Castle on the Hill

The theme of 'escapes gone wrong' was one of the most popular in cartoons in *The Camp*. 'No rest for the weary' was also a frequent theme.

CHAPTER 6

The Castle on the Hill

This time we weren't sent back to the work kommando but spent the rest of the summer of '43 in Molsdorf. During this period, tunnels were constantly being dug and discovered. Searches were constant and usually took place during the night. It was not unusual to be awakened two or three times nightly for head counts and searches for new tunnels. Snapping German police dogs were part of these visits and, although they were restrained by their leads, they often got too close for comfort.

During the searches, the boards were removed from the base of each hut so that the guards could see underneath the buildings, which stood on two-foot stilts. The ground was coated with lime to enable them to ascertain that the earth was undisturbed under the huts. This didn't stop the tunnels from being constructed though, for, during the night, earth was removed from beneath one hut or the other to start a hole, which was then cleverly concealed by a piece of plywood that had been removed from the walls of the hut. This was then covered with a coat of lime and lowered into place by four pieces of thread, each attached to a corner. As the hole was deepened, a man could be lowered into it and the plywood replaced over him, enabling the tunnelling to proceed in shift work.

The earth was hidden in the ceilings, which at times almost collapsed, and was finally disposed of by each man filling his pockets with dirt and then sprinkling it on the grounds of the camp, where it quickly became trampled into the earth by the ever moving prisoners.

Life was a never-ending battle of wits between the prisoners and the Jerrys. Punishment for a new tunnelling attempt was usually given by calling a parade and having the whole camp stand in the hot sun for hours on end without food or water. One day the camp Commandant called a parade to inform us, through an interpreter, how the war was progressing. It was a tale that we had heard often, telling us of how the brave German army had repulsed the enemy, leaving large numbers of our comrades dead. The prisoners' spontaneous reply was a loud and ringing cheer. The Commandant threw his hands up in disgust and told us that he would not give us any more news as we must be totally stupid to be cheering the death of our comrades. What he did not realize was that we were better informed than he, having our own methods of keeping abreast of the news.

Over and above the tunnels, individual escapes were attempted. One man calmly climbed over the wire in daylight, with rags wrapped around his hands for protection from the barbs. He was quickly apprehended and fortunately was not shot. Another, who took advantage of a new ditch being dug for the latrines, hid in the ditch and worked all night with only a spoon for a tool. He also was caught after a hard night's labour for nothing.

A trip wire, about a foot from the ground, ran completely around the inside perimeter of the camp. It was about twelve feet from the barbed-wire fence and no one was allowed to step over it on penalty of death. One day some prisoners were tossing a ball around when the ball went beyond the wire. One cool Canadian stepped nonchalantly over it to retrieve the ball, and the guard in the tower yelled a warning and squeezed off a short burst from his machine-gun. The prisoner unhurriedly retrieved the ball, gave the tower guard a disdainful look and stepped back over the wire to continue the game.

When we weren't tunnelling or plotting escape strategy, our time was spent in pleasant pastimes of our own devising or doing the less than pleasant tasks assigned us by the Jerrys.

One of the dirtier jobs that came up in rotation was the emptying of the latrines. These consisted of a long row of seats partly enclosed and set over a trench. Periodically, a 'honey-wagon' rolled in, drawn by a tired horse. It was a metal container equipped with a hose that was lowered into the trench. Our job was to handle the pump that removed the contents out of the ditch and into the wagon. The stench was horrible but what was worse was that when the container was filled an automatic device sucked the contents out and hurled them into the air over the barbed wire and into the fields beyond to be used as fertilizer for potatoes grown for the consumption of the prisoners. With any type of a wind, a good portion of the contents blew back in your face, the reason that most prisoners hid in their huts, except for the poor slobs on duty. I labelled this 'perpetual motion', as we ate the potatoes, disposed of them in a time-honoured fashion, then blew the residue over the field to help grow the potatoes that eventually found their way back into the camp again to be consumed.

On August 19, 1943, we held a short service to mark Dieppe's first anniversary. On August 28, I was sent to the hospital in

The workers (*Above*) and patients at the hospital for the blind in Haina showed remarkable courage and cheerfulness. The man in the centre of the front row was also expert at tattooing compasses on the thumbs of POWs dedicated to escape.

The variety of nationalities represented in the camp is evident in these photos rifled
from the files after liberation.

Arnstadt for recurring back trouble, my personal reminder of the raid. When the mortar exploded during the raid, a stone, thrown up by the blast, had hit me at the base of the spine. The injury was further aggravated by my being forced to lift too heavy a weight at Niederorschel. At the work kommando, I collapsed and was taken to the village doctor. I was held up between two prisoners while the doctor swung his arm to gain momentum and then brought his fist down on the top of my head. I yelled and fell as the pain hit my spine. His verdict was, 'No blood, no swelling, back to work!' Other prisoners in the camp covered for me by taking my work shifts and moving me from bed to bed as the shifts changed, a deed I'll never forget.

I wasn't back from Arnstadt very long when my eyeball got scratched with grit from the ever blowing dust. I was sent to the hospital in Haina, where the doctors applied drops. About a week later, my eye was still bad and again I went to Haina.

On this journey, I got a sense of the effect of the Allied bombing of Germany. While waiting for the train, a woman approached me on the platform and deliberately tried to spit in my face. I jumped back just in time but will never forget the look of intense hatred on her face. The guard just smirked and said nothing. On the train, I got nothing but glares of hostility and was glad to reach our destination. I could not believe that German prisoners in Canada would get this same hostility.

In the hospital, they discovered the scratch and special drops were put in each eye, one to dilate the injured eye and one to strengthen the other, or so I was led to believe. The trouble was that both eyes were dilated in error and my vision soon blurred to the point where I couldn't see. They assured me that my sight would be corrected in a few hours and shortly thereafter a blind POW escorted me to the blind ward for a temporary stay.

It was here that I learned of the remarkable courage of the sightless. It was bad enough to be imprisoned for an indeterminate period of time, but to be blind as well seemed to me to be just too much punishment for these men to take. All I could do was admire their dexterity and outward cheerfulness. There were a few tears shed, but only at night when they thought no one would know. It made me feel both ashamed of my minor ailment and thankful that I wasn't one of them.

I was interred here for ten days, even though my vision had returned to normal quite quickly. Each night I heard horrible screams coming from the next building, which I understood was

Edward Nash-Larkham and his "St. Dunstaner's Orchestra"

his, I should say, is the most unique band in any prison camp in Germany. Every
ember of this orchestra is blind, and belongs to the, "St. Dunstan's Blind Institute,"
ngland. They appear every six weeks at the stalag theatre, supported by variety turns
 other members of the school. All music is properly orchestrated by our music
teacher Sgt. R. Brown. N. Z. and who is a tremendous help to us all

This 1943 photo taken at Haina appeared in *The Camp*.

Of the many funerals at the camp, those for soldiers who
died in the salt mines occurred with depressing frequency.

an experimental hospital housing political prisoners. I couldn't learn too many details, but I did catch sight of some of the inmates during the day, pacing the guarded grounds in white and blue striped uniforms, the dress of a political prisoner. They were mostly Jewish, I was told.

One morning at dawn, when I got up to go to the latrine, I looked through the barred window and could see an army truck being loaded with apparently dead bodies, one on top of the other. They were all in striped uniforms. My first feeling at witnessing this macabre scene was one of horror, mingled with a touch of fear at the closeness of death. I closed my eyes and then opened them, hoping the scene would disappear, but no, it was still there and all I could do was watch with a dreadful and scary fascination.

This was the first indication I had of the atrocities that took place throughout Germany. The chilling horror and blind hopelessness of it stayed with me throughout the war and for a long time after.

On September 16, my eye having healed, I returned to Molsdorf and, on the 20th, the whole camp was moved in box-cars to a new prison building in Mühlhausen. This was called *Zweilager* (also 'the castle') and we were told that it was escape-proof and was for criminal POWs only.

At the station we were met by large bodies of guards and police and were marched under escort to our new quarters about two kilometres away. This was on a slight rise and at first sight was very different from the usual POW compounds. It was a large building, more like a jail, and was the Germans' answer to the many escapes and tunnels built at Molsdorf, which was badly undermined.

We entered through huge gates into a cobblestoned courtyard, lined up for the never-ending head count and were assigned to a dormitory that held about twelve men in double-decked bunks. There were three floors, with cells in the dungeons beneath, which were dark, damp and flea-infested. Overall, it was a nice change from the blowing dust in summer and the thick mud in winter of Molsdorf, but we realized that it would be very hard to escape from.

One of the first things I set out to do was find a suitable hiding place for my notes. On enlistment I had started a wartime diary. I kept notebooks covering my activities up to the time of Dieppe, and these were in a kit bag I left with relatives in Birmingham. From Dieppe to POW camp I continued the habit of taking notes, but it was hard to retain them. For instance, just before my first escape I left my notes in between layers of plywood in the bottom of a suitcase. This was left with a buddy who eventually destroyed it as he didn't think I would return. From that time on I hid my notes in linings, between walls, under floor boards, and in any niche I could find until the time came to retrieve them.

We received wartime logs from the war prisoners aid of the YMCA in Geneva, Switzerland, and most POWs started writing and keeping a daily log. Fortunately, I held off commencing mine until I could get my notes together. By fortunately I mean that after a few months the Germans confiscated the logs. When they were finally returned, any writing detrimental to the Third Reich was censored and warnings were issued about future writings.

From then on, the only items I carried on my person were my rice paper map, a compass and my official POW photo. The map was in my boot heel between two layers of leather, as previously mentioned, though another gimmick was to tie it in the knotted corner of an extremely soiled handkerchief. This worked over and over again, since when being searched the Germans, with a disgusted expression, would always push it gingerly aside with a stick or short baton.

The compass was in the form of two metal buttons sewn on my tunic; they were magnetized and a small 'white dot' on one button, denoting 'north', was the only difference from ordinary buttons. (Special thanks to an Air Force member!) The photo was hidden in the false bottom of a tin I used for carrying cigarette butts. This consisted of a small English 'Players' tobacco tin and an English cheese tin of slightly smaller diameter. The 'rolled' edge of the cheese tin hid the edge of the tobacco tin after insertion, and the 'Players' lid fitted perfectly over the edges of both tins.

We had barely become used to our new accommodation when we were temporarily shipped out again. A Red Cross Commission was due to arrive at the camp and choose men for repatriation. These were to be only DUs (definitely unfit for service), such as amputees, men with bad ulcers, the blind, etc., who would be sent home in a prisoner exchange. As more wounded arrived from Haina and Bad Sulza, on October 12, all except the DUs were evacuated in box-cars to Langen-Salza.

This was a hellish nightmare, as the cars were so overloaded that we could only stand shoulder to shoulder. As the freight moved, every man stumbled and shuffled his feet to maintain some balance. This caused the former contents of the box-car, powdered lime, to rise in eye-stinging and choking clouds. We yelled in vain, trying to attract the guards' attention. The ride seemed to be endless and, on reaching our destination, we emerged choking and spitting and with our uniforms covered in lime dust. We raised hell, but all those dumb bastards did was laugh in our faces.

The temporary building they herded us into was a two-storey affair. We were all put into the second storey, in overcrowded conditions. The windows, apart from being barred, were all boarded shut. There were no latrines, only a deep hole outside the building where groups were taken under guard. The hole was square and poles had been nailed to stakes for seating purposes. These poles were on all sides of the hole and, when you sat, you had an audience who could view you from every angle. This was not only embarrassing for even the toughest of prisoners but humiliating as well. If you had a hard time and were on the slow side, you heard shouts of derision to hurry it up. If you were fast, you received cheers of encouragement to get it over with and give the next man a chance.

On one occasion, there was a prisoner who was having a very difficult time. He was constipated. He looked sheepish and couldn't seem to get things going. Finally, with reddened face and bulging eyes, his efforts started to emerge. This started an extra loud cheer from the gallery. I swear the poor man inhaled deeply, his effort disappeared, and he relinquished his seat to the next victim.

If you were unfortunate enough to have to go at night, the only convenience was a huge hogshead on the bottom floor, with wooden steps leading up the side. This was at the foot of very steep stairs and at night the building was in total darkness, making it necessary to feel your way along. My first trip to the hogshead was, I hoped, my last. I managed to feel my way down the stairs and, with a sigh of relief, climbed the steps of the huge barrel. I just got my penis over the edge when a hand shot out of the darkness and grabbed it. I let out a blood-curdling yell, causing the unknown fag to drop it. I heard him scrambling up the stairs as the guards came running in, alerted by my cry. I tried to explain to them what had happened and they told me that, being a prisoner, I shouldn't have yelled out and that they thought I was crazy to complain. Instead, they claimed, I should have kept quiet and enjoyed it.

We returned to Mühlhausen on October 24, once again in sealed box-cars but, luckily, this time without the lime to add to our dis-comfort. The repatriation of the DUs had now been completed and we noticed, upon our arrival at the camp, that many familiar faces were missing. It made us feel sad and sorry for ourselves that we could not have gone with them but, on the other hand, we were happy that they were on the way home.

A few days later, there was a sign that the day of our going home might be getting closer. On October 31, a large group of Allied planes passed overhead. We had heard planes many times before, but on this day we could also hear the distant rumble of bombs falling on Kassel.

7:Passing the Time

Christmas
1943

To Canadian Prisoners Of War

Our Christmas gift of two pounds of chocolate and three hundred cigarettes has been despatched to you and we trust will arrive safely and in good time. The thoughts of your friends and relations and of all your countrymen are with you this Christmas time. The message we send you is one of hope and faith. Hope that the New Year will bring a speedy end to the separation and hardships of war. Faith in the future that we will build together. May the coming year bring you back to us and restore peace to the peoples of the World.

A Happy Christmas and A Happier New Year

Bertha Tobin Amelin

President

The Canadian Prisoners of War Relatives Association

1943 was the last Christmas we would receive the welcome package
from home.

CHAPTER 7

Passing the Time

On a cold day the following month, we were lined up for the usual morning roll call. We were called to attention as the Commandant strode into the camp for this twice-daily ritual. He was wearing his winter great coat that had a pale grey collar. The mousey fur around his fat face struck me as comical and I started to chuckle. As he passed down the line of prisoners and came directly in front of me, I couldn't hold it back any longer and started to laugh uncontrollably. He screamed something in German and his heavy jowls became livid in anger. Another guard, whom we had nicknamed 'Plank-face', took up the screaming and I was hauled out in front of the parade. I had a burning butt cupped in my hand and this was quickly noticed. They sentenced me to seven days in solitary and I was marched away immediately to the dungeon cells. This was on November 20, the day that 'Plank-face' became my deadly and hated enemy.

I took stock of my cell, which was about fifteen feet long and nine feet wide. The small barred window high on the wall looked out onto a stone exterior, and only a little daylight filtered in from above as the cell was underground. There was a wooden bunk without mattress or pillow. Two blankets were issued but only at night. The lone source of heat came from a small wood stove outside the cell door. This was usually unlit but, even when burning, the heat didn't get into the cell because the door was solidly constructed, except for a 'glass eye' that stared at you constantly.

I looked through the eye but drew a blank. I learned later that a guard, looking through the eye from the outside, could see the whole interior magnified when making his rounds of inspection. That was to become my means of aggravating 'Plank-face' on his four daily visits. I found that, by wetting my finger and rubbing it on the walls of the cell, I could smear the eye by coating it with whitewash.

The following morning, 'Plank-face' arrived with another guard who brought my daily jug of water and three slices of black bread. He ranted and raved at me but I acted dumb, letting my mouth hang open and repeating over and over 'Nixverstein' (*nichte verstehen*), a prisoner's regular method of getting out of trouble by pretending he didn't understand. I did understand his dire threats but, on every visit, when he found the eye smeared, I continued to act stupid and grinned at him until he got sick of me and finally gave up in disgust. He knew what I was doing but couldn't catch me at it.

He would try sneaking in at odd hours but, when you are in a cell by yourself, the slightest noise becomes magnified. I'd either hear his boots creak or sense that he was outside. Before he could enter, I'd yell 'Hello Plank-face, you ugly bastard, how are you today?'

He'd come rushing in and say in German, 'What is "Plank-face"?' and I'd reply, 'Nixverstein!' He hated my guts and I hated his. He was only an *Ober-gefreiter*, maybe a step above a lance-corporal, but he was a died-in-the-wool Nazi, a member of the Party. The other guards and even the Commandant seemed to fear him. We figured he was a Nazi stooge and informer. He was about six feet tall with thin stooped shoulders. His whole body was angular and bony. He had sunken baleful eyes set in a skull-like, evil face. His cheeks were hollow and the long etched crease lines extended down to the corners of his lips, pulling his mouth down into a perpetual surly expression. I hated the son-of-a-bitch.

On the third morning, after the guards' visit I kept hearing a voice calling my name. It was very faint and at first I thought it was my imagination but it continued and I tried to figure where it was coming from. Finally, I traced it to a small iron plate on the cell wall and, by tugging and pulling, I was able to remove the plate and reveal a soot clean-out space. The voice became clearer and when I put my ear to the space I could hear quite well.

It was the voice of a New Zealand sergeant, Jack Hinton, the only VC winner in our camp. He told me to hold my hand in the hole with palm up. I did so and, within seconds, a cigarette dropped into my palm, followed by a match. He was in the cell above me, which had a stove pipe inside it. By removing the clean-out plate from the pipe, he could put his hand in the opening and flick the cigarette past the elbow and into the flue, where it dropped into my cell. I believe he received the cigarettes from his combine, who bribed one of the friendly guards to pass them along. The cigarettes were a godsend but I had to blow the smoke into the flue, smoke the cigarette as low as possible and then grind the remains into the soot. Even with these precautions, 'Plank-face' would come in, sniff the air and accuse me of smoking. I'd just shrug as he searched me and the cell. He never did catch on to the method, so he couldn't charge me, which would have been an additional seven days confinement.

"MY RETREAT" (28 days) — MUHLHAUSEN 1944   (WALLACE) ORIGINAL

The view of the dungeon cell as seen by 'Plank-face' through the glass
eye in the door (when he could see through it).

Prisoners in solitary would be taken out three times a day. In the morning, we'd be taken to the latrine and then to the washrooms where we were locked in for fifteen minutes to wash and shave. We would always manage a quick smoke from butts that had been hidden in the ashes of the boilers by other prisoners. In the afternoons we'd get our exercise in a small yard completely surrounded by high walls. Here we would walk in small circles with our hands behind our backs. On one occasion, when I dropped my hands to my sides, 'Plank-face' yelled at me to get them behind my back. I didn't like being yelled at so I ignored him. He screamed in his usual insane manner and finally drew his pistol and threatened to shoot me. I stopped my circling and we stood glaring at each other as he again repeated his threat. I lost my temper and dared him to pull the trigger, called him all the rotten names I could think of and finishing the tirade by telling him that he didn't have the guts to shoot. The outburst was heard in the main camp and other guards came running in and stepped between us, pushing me to one side. There was a long discussion between the Germans as we resumed our circling. Our exercise period was cut short and we were returned to our cells.

I never heard anything further of the incident, but the next day I didn't receive my daily rations and another guard replaced 'Plank-face'. He was named Fritz and, unlike 'Plank-face', had seen front line action and was easier to get along with. He advised me not to cross 'Plank-face' as he was considered dangerous even by the other guards, who hated and feared him. I took the warning and decided to soft-pedal my harassment and ignore him, at least for the meantime!

At night we would be taken to the latrine around 9:30. Here, under cover of darkness, my combine would do their best to try and pass me some extra food. What with trying to go to the latrine and having the guard flashing his light on and off me, it was hard to consume very much. All I could usually manage was a couple of mouthfuls, which I had to chew between the flashes of light.

My seven days confinement seemed like a lifetime but finally it was behind me and I felt free again as I left my cell to rejoin my comrades in the main prison. They had a hot meal ready for me, prepared from my Red Cross parcel. The fried spam and biscuits were heaven, and so was the hot cup of tea followed by a chocolate bar and a cigarette. It seemed that the seven days were worth it just to come back to this.

The routine of daily life in prison passed slowly. At times it was boring and very discouraging. At other times there was the tinge of danger that made it exhilarating, but the things that made it possible to endure were the comradeship and unselfishness of most prisoners, along with the humour of daily happenings.

Included in these was our weekly trip to the showers where for a brief period you could feel liberated. There was lots of laughing and horseplay, especially if you dropped your soap and bent over to pick it up. The safest method was to get your back to a wall and slide down. Otherwise you were assured of being goosed and there was no guarantee of by what or by whom!

Weekend activities varied. On occasion we had dances where you tried to have fun without feeling too 'fruity'. If you danced with one partner too often, you soon became aware of sly glances and knowing whispers.

Poker and bridge were popular pastimes but the all-time favourite for many of us was 'horse racing', a board game introduced by the Aussies, where cigarettes were used for betting and literally thousands changed hands. When the originators were due for repatriation they turned the game over to those who were the deepest in debt, myself and two other Canadians. It didn't take long to clear our collective obligations but, before we were able to realize any profits, the Germans stepped in and closed the game down.

We held auctions where cigarettes or prison money served as cash. A bar of chocolate would bring 200 cigarettes, soap went for 50 and tooth paste or shoe polish would go for 100 cigarettes each. The highest priced item was a quarter-pound of tea. At one auction this brought 500 Reich marks in POW money, equivalent to 150 Canadian dollars.

During this period cigarettes were plentiful. We received them from home or from organizations in lots of 300 or 1,000. It was either feast or famine in the cigarette supply. You'd either be loaded or picking up butts if you'd lost at poker. If I played for cigarettes, I couldn't win. When I played for prison money, which I thought was worthless, I couldn't lose.

I used the money for toilet paper and occasionally for lighting twigs to brew a tin of water for tea. When I accumulated too much, I'd turn it over to the British confidant man, either for buying extra instruments through the Red Cross or for the escape fund. The last lot I turned in was about 3,000 marks, the largest amount I had won. The confidant man asked me why I didn't send some of it home. This was when I learned that each mark was worth 30 cents Canadian. I found it hard to believe but, when he insisted that this was the truth, I asked him to send 500 of the 3,000 marks to my mother, just as a test. Months later I received a thank you letter and I finally believed that the money was good. From then on, I couldn't win a mark, let alone a cigarette!

When the camp wasn't under punishment, we also had Saturday night concerts or boxing matches. Our camp band was well organized, with instruments received through the Red Cross, and its trumpeter kept the whole camp alive and laughing with his variety of tunes to let us know what was taking place. A few examples were: 'The Love Bug Will Get You' (MO inspection for vermin); 'Don't Tie My Hands, Let Me Wander' (chains on Canadians—a.m.); 'Deepest Shelter in Town' (air raid; to shelters); 'A Hunting We Will Go' (Gestapo search); 'Trees' (issue of brushwood for fires); 'Hold Your Hand Out You Naughty Boy' (camp punishment); 'Oh You Nasty Man' (when the Jerry known as 'Double Amp' was near); and 'Let's Put Out The Lights And Go To Sleep' (lights out, 10:00 p.m.).

The trumpet was just one means of passing on information. We existed on rumours and the favourite question was, 'What's the "prop" today?' (Propaganda). If the news was encouraging, we were elated for days on end. If bad, when the Allies suffered reverses, we suffered with them and felt fits of depression. Fortunately, the men soon bounced back and in time learned to roll with the punches. Inwardly, we knew that we would eventually win and it was just a case of existing and staying alive until the big day arrived.

Every day, a British NCO would visit each room and call out, 'News Time'. He was the runner who would bring us the latest word from the BBC. We never knew where the wireless was located, how it was obtained, or who operated it, but we were always grateful for the service.

We would also get information from men sent into town to unload box-cars, who would then have quiet conversations with the French train engineers. Scraps of information came from prisoners transferred from other camps, too. In this way we heard that a Canadian had been shot and killed when trying to escape from a strafe camp. Another had purposely held his thumb on a rock in the stone quarry and had persuaded another prisoner to hit it with a sledge hammer in order to get out of work. His thumb was amputated and he had a few months' rest in the hospital, then was sent back to work. We learned of men killed while attempting to escape, others killed in salt mine cave-ins and still others sentenced to hard labour in Poland for sabotage or striking their guards. We also heard of the mass murder of Polish officers in Katyn forest.

One day we heard a strange and unfamiliar noise in the sky. We knew it was some type of aircraft but we could never catch sight of it. It was some time before we learned that this was the new jet aircraft the Germans had developed. It was the second 'new' thing that I had seen as a prisoner, the first being the chain saw that I had used in the work kommando to cut logs.

These people, if nothing else, were resourceful. They had trucks which ran on wood instead of gasoline, using small square blocks of wood which were burned in a boiler on the back of the trucks. I didn't know the principal on which they worked, but they did run. Then there was the ersatz coffee we drank, which I understood was made from acorns, and the black bread, which looked as if it was covered in sawdust. On enquiry, I was told that it *was* sawdust!

In the wood factory I had worked in, the stoves burned sawdust. This was packed wet into a double-walled cylinder and, when lit, it burned with a blue flame. There wasn't a lot of heat, but they did work. (We supplemented the heat by burning our bed boards. The only thing wrong with this was that, when you burnt too many, the straw palliasse fell through to the bunk underneath.)

Aside from being resourceful, though, the Germans were also either very stupid or single-minded. For example, during the constant Gestapo searches, if they were looking for knives, they would ignore some other forbidden item. One day, during a surprise search, they came tearing in looking for guns. I was lying on my bunk, looking over my map, trying to figure which way to go on some future escape. They threw the map to the floor and proceeded to slit my palliasse wide open, strewing the straw every which way. They tore the place apart but the map was left lying there. This search was successful for them but only by accident. Most of the Gestapo had left when one of the accompanying guards walked across the courtyard and, in ducking under the line of underwear and socks hanging in the yard, he banged his head on a sock with a pistol concealed in the toe. He rubbed his head but continued on his way. All of a sudden he stopped as it gradually dawned on him that a sock should not be so hard. He was the hero of the day and the whole camp was put on strafe (punishment).

The punishment for that episode was that every last man was ordered to sew and mend all day. This was a very light and stupid

✓ Smoking on Parade or in bed — 7 days close arrest   (in cells on Bread & Water)

Not carrying identity disk   "

✓ Refusing to go to Air Raid shelter   "

✓ Laying on bed in day time   "

Improper dress on parade   "

Expectorating or throwing rubbish on the square   "

✓ Escape or attempted escape   —   21 days close arrest — shot if seen in act.

Stepping over trip-wire or out of bounds   —   a shot !

✓ Cutting wires or digging tunnels   —   'collective punishment' such as, being kept on parade all day — sewing parade — continuous turnouts & searches — roll calls two or three times during the night etc..etc.

✓ Refusing to work   —   Rifle butts or one to two years in Poland

Striking civilian or civil guards   —   six months to two years

Striking German military guard   —   usually shot on spot

✓ Dealing or trading with German civilians   —   six months or more for P.O.W. — Prison for civilian

✓ Talking politics

Having intercourse —   woman   —   up to 10 years imprisonment (death penalty can be given) (prison or death for woman)

✓ Sabotage   —   Two years or more

✓ Ridiculing - insulting or writing matter against the German army or nation   —   one month or more close arrest

The above are among the charges that can be imposed on a P.O.W. — 21 day charges are served in cells, on bread & water (4 x 24) — or in Strafe camp (Stone quarry)

Other charges or sentences, are served in Poland Strafe Camps where the work is harder and food parcels & cigarettes are only issued fort nightly instead of weekly

The more serious charges of Sabotage or Intercourse with German women are served in civil prison where no parcels or cigarettes are received.

(short sentences given "on spot" - no trial)

The British P.o.W. no —— is 'awarded', 21 days close arrest etc.

Gericht de Kommandeurs der Panzertruppen - Erfurt 20 Sept. '44

air Oppeln - 15/8/44 - Cpl. Thomas Coutts - etc. etc. - is accused of being
sufficiently suspected of having publicly tried to lame & to undermine
the will of military self-defence of the German people - etc.

Evidence - Cpl. Coutts was greeted by a German woman (who did not know he
was a foreigner) - with 'Heil Hitler' - He replied - "What Heil Hitler.
I do not Heil Hitler - nothing to eat - no clothing & still Heil Hitler.
It must be Heil Roosevelt. When the Bolshevists are coming, then
Germany goes to America. The German girls must marry Americans.
In Germany everything is sad. In America all is gay & dancing - etc.

Sentence - one year

Gericht der Division

Kassel 4.8.1943   (BUCKY)

Bill of Indictment

The British P.o.W. Wm. Buchanan Pte. no. 324 is accused of being sufficiently
suspected of having disobeyed official orders at Sömmeroda & then purposely
causing considerable injury in War time.
Evidence - although Buchanan knew the ordinance of the O.K.W., whereby it is
forbidden to approach German women - etc. - He took up close relations with mrs.
Gärtner. He talked to her oftener & was leading political conversations with her.
Therefore mrs. G. brought once a larger map with her at which they had a look
together. In may/43, he called mrs. G. being in his lodgings, to her window &
asked her to throw the map down. This, mrs. G. did. Buchanan took the map
& put it into the inner side of his coat & went away. In June/43 he conversed
again with mrs. G. in presence of some craftsmen, & made some contemptuous remarks about
Germany.

Sentence: 4 months

Court of 40g Division   Kassel 27 Jan/42 .

Pte. Geo. Raines - He is sufficiently suspected of having carried out his criminal intentions on the 15th Dec./41, at the Kali Works of Sollstedt to disorganize or endanger the regular working of a plant which is important for the defence of the Reich or the maintenance of the population by making completely or partially useless one of the devices of great importance to the plant.

Evidence:- The accused in his work at the mine pushes cars, empty & full from termination to the chain & back ths whilst changing shifts the defendant picked up a piece of iron about 30 Cm. long & threw it into an empty car, which was on the way to the termination - (Witness Kunze). Breakdowns have occurred frequently at the above named plant, caused by iron found among potash ready for grinding. (Defence was that he had threw it into said car thinking it to be the one for scrap iron) - Sentence - 2 Years Hard Labour.

Erfurt —— /44

Pte. Harding - accused of having close relations with ——— who assisted him to escape by supplying him with German money, a map, railway ticket & civilian clothing.

Sentence 3 Years - (woman 10 years Prison)

Court of Div. 409   Erfurt 25/2/44   (Pte.)

Decree of Punishment

The British P.o.W. Robert Savage Sgt. 42887 at Zweigler, Mühlhausen, is punished with four weeks close-confinement for insulting his superior!

Statement of Case

The Obergefreite Heitmann patroled the camp during an Anti-Aircraft Alarm, on the 20/2/44 at 2.30 P.m. He thereby noticed that several P.o.W. stayed outside the Air Raid Shelter. When H. ordered them to go into the shelter, Savage called Heitmann "Du Schweinehund" - Heitmann asked Savage "who, me?" - Savage answered yes.

Sentence 4 months close confinement

punishment but I believe it was meant to ridicule us, as we had to do the mending in the courtyard under the eyes of the Germans.

I could see 'Gee-guts', the Commandant, (sometimes also known as 'Lard-ass') laughing as he watched the procedure from his office window. What made it galling was that as he stood there he was eating the bully-beef from one of our Red Cross parcels. He calmly cut pieces out with his knife and shoved them in his ugly fat face.

We did our best to get back at the guards in any way we could. Crazy humour was rampant and I fully believe the Jerrys thought we were all nuts. Prisoners went out of their way with inane gestures and silly antics to confuse them and the Germans often had a blank or confused look and appeared unable to make head or tail out of the insane activities of their captives.

The guards loved Canadian cigarettes and, when they were plentiful (after receiving a carton from home), a favourite trick was to light-up in front of a guard, take a couple of puffs, then throw the cigarette at his feet. You could see his eyes widen, waiting for you to move on so that he could retrieve the large butt. Instead, you would grin at him, step forward and grind it under your heel. Cruel maybe, but effective, as we were the prisoners and they, our captors and so-called superiors, who knew of Germany's shortages and, through us, knew of the riches of our homeland.

Some of our guards were as fed up with the war as we were, especially those who had seen frontline action. These men, usually having been wounded, were given POW camp duties and plainly disliked the job. In conversation, their favourite expressions were, 'Keine essen, keine zigarette, alles kaput'. (Nothing to eat, no cigarettes, all is ruined!) All they wanted was to get the war over and return to their families.

As in all nations, there were the good, the bad and the absolutely rotten. For example, there was 'Schmid' (or 'Smitty'). He was extremely short and had a ruddy cherubic face and a perpetual grin. He looked like a miniature Santa Claus and could even be classed as 'cute'. When other guards weren't around he tried to be friendly, and some prisoners slipped him the odd free fag for trying to be nice. Then there was 'Fritz'. He sported a glass eye, and delighted in ordering prisoners around when other guards were within hearing, but on his own he was strictly on the take and could be bribed for favours. For the third type, I'll just say, 'Plank-Face'.

Very few of the guards or officers could give an order quietly.

They had to scream their instructions, a continuous repetition of *'Raus'* (short for *heraus*) and *'Schnell machen'*, literally, 'Get out and make it fast'. Most prisoners muttered 'FO', in response!

I had my eyes on one of the guard's ribbons and, being an avid collector, I tried on several occasions to brush against him and 'acquire' the ribbon that had miniature crossed swords affixed. Having no success, I offered him a few cigarettes in trade and was surprised when he promptly accepted and handed me the souvenir. Another item I collected by the same method was a 'Death's Head' ring. This particular guard seemed over-anxious to trade and I got it for ten cigarettes. I don't believe the ring really belonged to him. The reason for my assumption was that this insignia (a skull) was only worn by the *Waffen-SS Totenkopf Verbande* or Death's Head Units, the infamous collection of professional soldiers under the direct command of Himmler. Being 'fighting' soldiers, they would not be classed as criminals, like the SS (*Schutz-Staffeln*—Nazi Party Troops), the SD (*Sickerheits-dienst*—Security Service), or even the Gestapo (*Geheime Staats-polizei*—political police force), but many unlawful acts were attributed to them, such as the shooting of unarmed prisoners, massacres and other atrocities.

Prisoners of war were aware that among the camp staff there was always one or sometimes two Gestapo or SD men present, usually with ears tuned in for anything political or racial being said against Germany. They spoke perfect English and acted as interpreters, officially, but were there for other purposes and were always trying to engage prisoners in conversation. The majority of prisoners smelled a rat and would not have anything to do with them and their oily manner.

The plain-clothed Gestapo, who conducted the periodic searches, were something else. You could spot them a mile away with their long black leather coats and their stubby Hitler moustaches. They'd come charging in with a bunch of guards and literally tear the place apart. They would very seldom find anything, as usually we'd get tipped-off ahead of time by bribed guards. If they hadn't been so sinister, they would have been comical, as they all looked alike, just like a bunch of cloned Hitlers.

On the POW side, variety was the rule. In a camp the size of ours, you mingled with all types of men. Name a trade or occupation and we had it. There were electricians, carpenters, tinsmiths, loggers, miners, etc., etc. The camp could produce men who could pick any lock or remove the gold fillings from your teeth.

We had musicians, actors, poets and some very good artists and cartoonists. There were cultured and well-educated men and men who didn't know their rear ends from a hole in the ground. There were lawyers and doctors, excellent surgeons, plus a few titled men, all intent on doing their bit in adversity.

British 'regulars', hardened to army life in Egypt or India, seemed to have a quiet air of endurance and patience. Some would sit knitting for hours on end as others strummed away on banjos or any instrument they could get their hands on. We even had a pipe major who practised constantly on a chanter (used by pipers for bagpipe practice—the Germans called them 'doodle-sacks'). 'Pipey', as he was affectionately called, was respected by all. This was fortunate, as the plaintive notes drove us 'bananas'.

Among the other characters, there was 'Nick', a garrulous individual and not extremely popular. His redeeming feature was his ability to act. He took part in some of the camp plays and immediately became the person he was portraying. His acting was so good, he amazed the prisoners, who usually gave him a standing ovation despite their personal feelings about him. 'Bucky' was a miniature scoundrel, short, dark and handsome in a rough-and-tough-looking way. He had a perpetual grin and was a born scrounger. In other words, if you wanted something, ask Bucky and he would produce it. 'Sinc' was a very gentle man who should never have been in the army. He was poetic, well-educated, well-mannered, and exuded kindness and compassion. 'Lard-ass' (not to be confused with the Commandant) was fat, bloated and greedy, a real life Billy Bunter of the *Gem* and *Magnet* type of English school magazines.

In one of the other camps, there was the heir to a prominent British millionaire. I was told that during the march into captivity after the Battle of Dunkirk, this private had given IOUs for race horses he owned in trade for bread rations. I heard later, after release, that he had honoured these debts! Although this is only hearsay, I was inclined to believe it. After the war, I read an article describing this man's exploits in post-war England, the main gist of which was that he had squandered his fortune in 'high-living' and 'give-aways' to former comrades. The story ended by saying that he was broke but happy. With his last pounds he had purchased a horse-drawn wagon, stocked it with pots and pans and was living a gypsy-type existence travelling and selling across the countryside.

In our combine, we had a good group of guys who shared every-

"Rugby Union"

(as played in England, New Zealand, Australia & South Africa)

Mühlhausen - 20/3/44

Great Britain

vs.

Dominions

Dominions

Dominions		Position	Great Britain
SGT. JACK HINTON - V.C. - NEW ZEALAND		FULL BACK	SGT. ANDY SKYRME - WALES
PTE. WANA (MAORI)	" "	MIDDLE ROW (LOCK)	" KNOBBY CLARKE - YORKSHIRE
" SNOWY MACKIE	" "	SCRUM HALF	CPL. JIM OAKLEY - HAMPSHIRE
SGT. CLEM GRAFF	" "	WING 3/4	CPL. GINGER BOYER. YORKSHIRE
PTE. LARRY GIBBS	" "	"	" JOE GREEN - LONDON
CPL. PHIL BOSHOFF	SOUTH AFRICA	BACK ROW	SGT. DENIS GALLAGHER - LEICESTER
PTE. GILDEA	" "	MIDDLE ROW (LOCK)	" JOE O'BRIEN - SUNDERLAND
CPL. BILL LISSON	CANADA	" " (BREAKAWAY)	PTE. HARVAY - LANCASHIRE
CPL. BOB PROUSE	"	" " "	CPL. NIBLETT - WALES
SGT. ED. HEATH	"	FRONT ROW	" DENIS ROE - DERBY
PTE. BUSSOON	SOUTH AFRICA	" (HOOKER)	SGT. DANDY McLAINE - SCOTLAND
" DIGGER BURKE	AUSTRALIA	SECOND 5/8	PTE. TOMMY BARTON - WOLVERHAMPTON
" FRED LYONS	CANADA	CENTRE 3/4	CPL. " PARKER - YORKSHIRE
SGT. McKENZIE	"	FRONT ROW	PTE. WOODLANDS - IRELAND
PTE. TOMMIE TAYLOR	NEW ZEALAND	FIRST 5/8 (FLY HALF)	SGT. FRED COLLINS - LONDON

Dominions 3 - Great Britain 0

14/4/44	0	9
14/7/44	6	0
2/11/44	6	18
18/2/45	3	0

NUTTALL - NEW ZEALAND
SAVAGE - CANADA
ARTHURS - NEW ZEALAND
JOE SIMPSON - "

CAPT. HINSLEY (PADRE) - LONDON
SGT. JOE GREENAWAY - "
TAYLOR - " "
ELLIOT - " "

"WEATHER - STRAFE + R.A.F. PERMITTING"

"GROUSE IN JUNE" - 3 ACT FARCICAL COMEDY - 5-6, FEB. 1944

"LORD PETER IN THE PANTRY" - " - "

"YOUTH AT THE HELM" - " - " 17 JUNE, 1944

"GASLIGHT" - 3 ACT VICTORIAN THRILLER - 12,13 AUG. 1944

"KING'S MARCH" - 1 - XMAS PLAY (BIBLICAL) - 24 DEC. 1944

"GRAND HOTEL" - MUSICAL VARIETY

"IN TOWN TONIGHT" - " - "

"FUMED OAK" - 1 ACT COMEDY (RADIO PLAY)

"HEWERS OF COAL" - 1 - DRAMA " - "

"M. AND V." - MUSICAL VARIETYS

BRASS BAND - DICK TANNER AND HIS BRITANNIQUES

STRING BAND - "DON ADAMS - " MANDOLIERS"

Above : The effort put into the staging of dramas and musical reviews enlivened life in the camp.

Left : Good-humoured rivalry between Great Britain and the dominions of Canada, Australia, New Zealand and South Africa was played out in a five-game series of rugby matches.

thing equally, including private parcels from home or anything scrounged. There was only one exception, an over-weight character who worked in the camp kitchen. This no doubt supplied him with extra grub which enabled him to maintain his enormous bulk, an exception to the rule in normal POW life. I wasn't too fond of him but at times, when I felt exceptionally hungry, I'd catch myself staring longingly at his fat arms, wondering what they'd taste like sliced in inch-thick steaks and fried to a turn. I knew I'd never stoop to this but I have to admit that I did get a great deal of satisfaction from imagining it!

On more than one occasion when we had run out of our meagre ration of sugar, we would notice him sneaking something from under his bottom bunk and slipping it into his cup of ersatz coffee. The rest of us discussed the matter and decided to search under his bunk after he had left the room for kitchen duty. Sure enough, we found a parcel he had received from home containing sugar and other small luxuries. He hadn't mentioned it and had kept it hidden from other members of the combine. Since we shared everything, including home parcels, we confiscated what was left and had ourselves a party. The most enjoyable part of the episode was watching the look on his face when he returned from duty and found the parcel missing. We didn't let on that anything was wrong and he couldn't say a word without giving himself away.

One of the other Canadians had a voracious appetite. He was a one-man combine himself and always ate his Red Cross parcel issue in one sitting. He wolfed it down and, being forever hungry, he was always on the prowl for anything edible that could be scrounged or stolen. He even stole the potatoes we had to sort.

Potato sorting was a chore everyone disliked. We took turns going to the storage cellar located underground in the middle of the compound. The entrance was covered with a locked man-hole cover which led down a steep ladder to the storage area where the potatoes were laid on crated boards to allow the air to circulate. It was our job to inspect the potatoes, weed out the rotten ones, of which there were plenty, and re-stack the remainder. When I say rotten potatoes, I mean putrid. They were black and squishy and fell apart in your hands, a soggy rotten pulp.

After his first stint in the potato cellar, it didn't take our one-man combine long to pick the padlock on dark nights, remove the man-hole cover and load his blouse-like army tunic. How he managed on his own to escape being seen by the ever-prowling guards was beyond me, but do it he did, and successfully!

This man was quite a character, a loner and tough as nails. He was forever getting into fights, just for the love of it, and never seemed to be without a black eye. It became a kind of a trade-mark. He was pugnacious but he had a certain child-like guile that made him likeable. On one occasion, when he was locked up in solitary for some infraction of rules, we were being herded down the dungeon-like stairs to the air-raid shelters. On passing his cell, he suddenly stepped out with the cell door in his arms and asked what all the commotion was about. He was promptly locked up again and, after serving his time, wouldn't reveal how he had removed the heavy door. Being on a bread and water diet, it wouldn't have surprised me if he had made nightly forays to the potato cellar to satisfy his enormous appetite even while in strict solitary confinement.

With such an odd assortment of characters, it was difficult to get too depressed during the long camp days, but after 'lights out' you were on your own. Sometimes it was a pleasant escape from reality, a release into the dreamland of good food, wine, women and song. My main dream never varied—it was always bacon and eggs followed by ice cream. But there could also be loneliness, as I

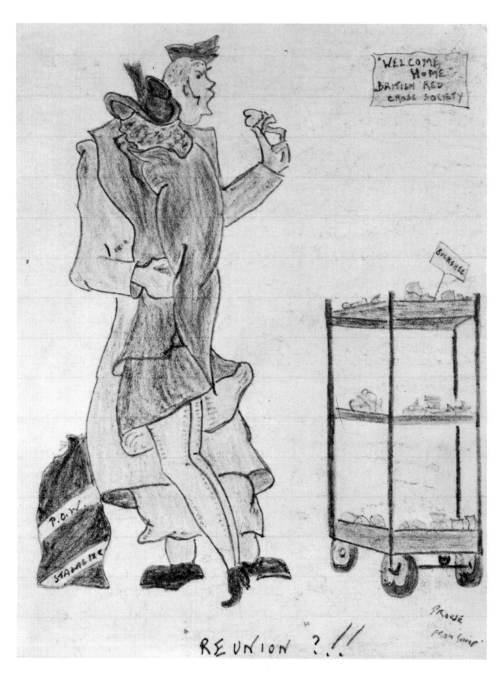

Prisoners were hard pressed to decide which fantasy took precedence:
the feel of a woman's arms around them or the taste of good food.

dreamed of my wife or of women who remained faceless and elusive.

The weekends were the worst, especially on Sundays, when German soldiers would walk their girls past the building. The girls would invariably look up to the prisoners peering at them through the bars and flirt openly. This would start a chorus of wolf whistles that enraged the girls' escorts, who would hurry them away. We would all laugh, but just the sight of the pretty girls would leave us with a hunger that increased the loneliness.

A few soldiers couldn't wait for freedom and indulged in homosexuality. Fortunately, they were a very small minority but disturbing all the same when you realized that some were otherwise tough soldiers. It made you wonder if you, too, could be affected someday if the war went on endlessly. Although the thought was revolting to most, it had to make one ponder the long-term effect of prison on a person's character. I felt sure that part of the problem was started by one man in our midst. He wasn't even a soldier but a member of the Navy, Army and Air Force Institution (NAAFI) that ran servicemen's canteens during the war. The story went that during the Battle of Dunkirk and just before capture, this man discarded his NAAFI uniform and obtained an officer's uniform from one of the dead, hoping to receive better treatment as a prisoner. Eventually ending up in Oflag (officer's camp), he was quickly discovered. He then claimed that he was a corporal and was placed in the NCO camp.

It was soon ascertained that he was homosexual and he became a camp fixture. The man was extremely clean, good looking and well built, in a slender way. It was common knowledge that he took very good care of his 'love' of the moment, doing his washing and serving his every need, within the scope of prison life. I only had one brush with him, when visiting the camp medical room situated in the lower corridors. He brushed against me in passing, seized my wrist and whispered, 'I'd like to get to know you better.' I tried to free my wrist and was amazed at his strength and grip. I then told him that if he didn't let go and bugger off, I'd knock his teeth down his throat. His smiling reply was, 'Would you do that, Bob? I'd just love it!' He didn't release my wrist, so I lost my temper and slammed him against the stone walls, knocking the wind out of him. I didn't wait around and hurried away. He never spoke to me again and looked right through me in passing, for which I was grateful. We badly needed fresh fruit in prison but certainly not of that sort.

Other soldiers found different alternatives. Once, we received a medicine ball from the Red Cross and it was much appreciated as an instrument of exercise. Unfortunately, an individual had other nefarious designs on it and the ball was found to be missing. It was eventually discovered in the drying room used for hanging our washing but something had happened that had ruined the ball's character. A hole had been punched into the downy innards and we discovered very good reasons to believe a Casanova had made it the object of his affections! Evidently, desperation breeds desperate measures in some cases but fortunately they were few.

An honour guard of German soldiers fire a *feu de joie* for yet another victim of the salt mines at Bischofferode.

8: The War
Catches Up

Peterhof "Pfefferode, Germany

Above : The *Peterhof Gasthaus* was a
welcome refuge from the
atmosphere of the camp and the
drudgery of the work parties.

Right : Often the POWs would
barely make it back to their bunks
before the unholy wail of the air-
raid siren was heard again.

CHAPTER 8

The War Catches Up

On New Year's Day, 1944, hundreds of planes passed overhead and the air-raid sirens began to wail. There was the sound of machine-gun fire as the fighters engaged in dogfights. We were herded into the dungeons, which served as air-raid shelters, and immediately were attacked by hordes of fleas. They made life miserable and I vowed to do everything I could to keep out of the shelters in future raids.

I avoided retreating to the shelters for quite a long period. First I hid between the blackout board and the bars on the window. When this was discovered, I tried hanging half of my body over the inside edge of my top bunk and pulling a blanket over myself and the edge of the bunk. This worked for a long time until an enterprising guard stood on the edge of the bottom bunk and prodded the blanket with his rifle butt.

I spent hours devising means of concealment, only to have one after the other discovered. Each time I'd receive the butt of a rifle for my efforts and finally the time arrived when I ran out of hiding places and had to join the others in the dark and damp cellars. What made these trying periods worse was not having food or drink, as we could not leave the shelters until the all-clear siren was sounded. Often, we would have just got out and sighed with relief when the siren would blare again and we'd have to go back down.

The planes passed over night and day, and while watching the many dogfights overhead, with planes tumbling from the sky, trailing black smoke, I was reminded of the Battle of Britain. In those days in England, it had been a pleasure to watch as our boys beat the hell out of the German Air Force. Now there was a feeling of apprehension. We were really happy to see them but having your own side drop bombs nearby leaves you with a helpless feeling.

The raids continued throughout the spring and seldom a day passed without the sirens forcing us to the underground shelters. Hundreds of planes were constantly overhead, headed for the big cities to drop their loads. Now and then the building would shudder as disabled bombers jettisoned their bombs in the nearby fields.

It was a trying time and hard on the nerves, not only because of the raids. The German rations for POWs had been cut back and the food situation was getting serious. Some prisoners rummaged through the kitchen garbage pails for potato peelings or any other scraps of food. A notice was posted by the senior officer to cease this practice, as it was beneath the dignity of British soldiers. The order had a sobering effect and most of the hungry prisoners obeyed and tightened their belts over their rumbling stomachs.

In early April, word came through the grapevine that seventy-six air force officers had made a mass escape from Stalag Luft. III. The escape was effected in March and later we heard that fifty of the prisoners had been shot and killed after recapture. The Germans stated that some of the men had resisted recapture and others had tried to re-escape while being transported back to prison camp. These were German lies to cover up out-and-out murder. We knew there was no way that so many men would act so foolishly or try to escape on the spur of the moment. At a later date we heard that most of the remaining escapees had been returned to the prison camp, except for three men who had somehow managed to get away.

This event made us realize fully just how ruthless these bastards could be. We had always known that escaping was dangerous and that being shot and killed while in the act was a possibility, a risk you took. What was so hard to swallow was the shooting of unarmed soldiers after recapture. We knew it could happen, especially if someone was caught by SS men or the ruthless Hitler Youth fanatics, but we dismissed it from our minds and honestly felt that it wouldn't happen to us. What we didn't know until after the war was that Hitler had issued an order on March 4, 1944, called the 'Bullet Decree', which stated in part that recaptured prisoners 'other than British or American' were to be turned over to the SD for execution.

It also wasn't until after the war that I learned of the concentration and death camps throughout Germany and other occupied countries, even though Buchenwald, one of the more notorious, was situated only seventy kilometres from our camp in Mühlhausen. Ironically, Buchenwald was only five or six miles from Weimar, a shrine of German culture and 'freedom', and Weimar itself was in central Germany adjacent to Jena and Erfurt. I had been in all of these towns little realizing the degradation and inhumanity that went on not too many miles away.

I had seen the starved skeleton-like Russian soldiers in Stalag VIG and I'd witnessed the loading of political prisoners' bodies at Haina, but on reading the atrocious history of this particular camp—the beatings and the starvation of its inmates, the barbarous acts of 'head-shrinking' and the collecting of skin bearing tattoos from murdered prisoners so the commandant's wife could make the skin into lamp shades and book covers—I find it hard to believe that we prisoners never heard a whisper of what took place there. But the fact remains that this was the case.

On June 5, a British POW, one of the originals held since Dunkirk, calmly walked through the open gates as the potato wagon rumbled in. The surprised guard watched him with mouth agape, not believing his own eyes. He finally realized what was happening and let out a yell, alerting the others in the nearby guard house. They came tumbling out and raced down the road after the fleeing prisoner. We figured that to walk out in broad daylight, right under their noses, was a spur of the moment act of sheer desperation brought on by the long incarceration and the increasing tension within the camp. After about two hours, the man was dragged back to the camp, bleeding from the ear and the side of the head, where he had been beaten with rifle butts. That evening, he was taken to the hospital and we learned later that he escaped from there and was killed under a moving train.

On June 6, we heard the welcome news that the Allies had landed in France, creating a second front. This was the first really encouraging news in months and it gave the whole camp a new feeling of hope. That same month, thirty-five Canadians in the camp received their first ribbons, the CVSM (Canadian Volunteer Service Medal for eighteen or more months overseas). Being our first medal, we wore it proudly and got the feeling that we hadn't been completely forgotten. These two events were the only positive ones, however, at that time.

With all the activity, news, rumours and propaganda, I had completely forgotten the consequences of my escapes. This was brought home to me on June 26, when I received a sentence of twenty-one days' solitary confinement, on bread and water, for my first escape. With the experience of the seven days that I had served previously still fresh in my mind, I wasn't looking forward to being locked up again. There was nothing I could do about it though, and on July 9 I began serving my sentence.

This time I put salt in all of my pockets to sprinkle on the black bread to make it taste a little better. It's wonderful what the

Finding and loading tree stumps was hard work, and it was not made any easier when the horse died and we had to haul the load ourselves.

Padre Bamber, a British chaplain, was a fine artist who captured the tranquility of Peterhof in this pen sketch.

imagination can accomplish. With the help of the salt I could close my eyes and turn the bread into different tasty dishes. I'd try steak one day and pork chops the next. After a few trial runs the bread actually tasted like whatever I imagined it to be.

Alone in the cell, the time seemed endless and the only really active thing was my mind. I would go back in time and relive my fondest memories. I would concoct wild plans of escape and let my imagination run wild. I was allowed books as they became available, but most of them were missing pages and were dog-eared and torn. My main pastime was writing poetry, or at least doggerel, and breaking down the days into minutes and seconds to keep in mind how long it would be before I finished my sentence.

I tried not to aggravate 'Plank-face' on his duty days, especially since he kept threatening to get me sentenced to an extra seven days whenever he could smell smoke. I was careful not to get caught smoking the few cigarettes that had been smuggled to me, but I just couldn't resist smudging the eye in the door with whitewash. He still couldn't catch me in the act.

My hips got sorer with each passing day from sleeping on the bare boards and I had a constant stiff neck from my pillow of two books. Every third day, according to regulations, I was given a hot bowl of soup, either cabbage or potato. It wasn't much but it was the only event to look forward to. The only good thing about my stay was that I didn't have to jump up at night to go to the air-raid shelters during the continuing heavy raids.

My big worry was that I had another sentence of twenty-one days hanging over my head for the second escape. I tried to dismiss it from my thoughts. I dreaded this period of being absolutely alone, when the mind starts playing funny tricks. Could I take it? That question was uppermost in my head. At the end of the month, I was released from my cell and was elated that I still had all of my marbles!

Shortly thereafter, new Canadian prisoners began to arrive in camp for the first time since Dieppe. They were from a parachute regiment dropped over Arnhem, and from what we could learn the drop was less than a success. They were welcomed to a less than happy camp.

Later, we received news over the short-wave set that Anthony Eden, in a recent speech, had condemned the Germans for murdering escaping POWs. The German answer was to post a notice on our bulletin board stating that German civilians would shoot and kill any escaping prisoner, in revenge for the heavy

Being out in the woods in the middle of winter brought back many
memories of cold, quiet days on the ski slopes of Quebec.

bombing of their cities. The next day we heard that two prisoners had been killed for assaulting a guard and two others while attempting escape. It was evident that the Jerrys were getting jumpy with the constant bombing and with the knowledge that the Allies were starting to turn the tide. Another notice went up stating that we would be shot without warning if we left our rooms at night or stepped over the trip wire in the daytime.

Letters were received in the camp from the DUs repatriated to England. They advised us that two of their number had been court-martialled, one receiving two years for collaborating with the Germans and another ten years for the same offence as well as for impersonating an officer while a prisoner of war. I knew of at least two more who would meet their own fate when we got out of this!

August 19, 1944, the second anniversary of Dieppe, was celebrated with a three-hour air raid and the news of two more escapees reaching the French border only to be shot and killed. On September 10, as the air raids continued, two fighter planes were shot down and crashed nearby and bombs fell on the town of Mühlhausen, killing ten civilians. On the 12th, more bombs hit the town and thirty more were killed. Giving the heavy bombing as a reason, the Germans cut our Red Cross parcels to a half parcel a week. We took this to be good news. The planes were hitting their depots and marshalling yards.

During this period, a leaflet circulated throughout the POW camps showed that the Jerrys definitely had the wind up. The leaflet declared:

'As a result of repeated applications from British subjects from all parts of the world, wishing to take part in the common European struggle against Bolshevism, authorization has recently been given for the creation of a British volunteer unit.

The British Free Corps publishes herewith the following short statement of the aims and principles of the unit.

1. The British Free Corps is a thoroughly British volunteer unit, conceived and created by British subjects from all parts of the empire, who have taken up arms and pledged their lives in the common European struggle against Soviet Russia.

2. The British Free Corps condemns the war with Germany and the sacrifice of British blood in the interests of Jewry and international finance, and regards the conflict as a funda-

mental betrayal of the British people and British Imperial interests.

3. The British Free Corps desires the establishment of peace in Europe, the development of close friendly relations between England and Germany and the encouragement of mutual understanding and collaboration between the two great Germanic peoples.

4. The British Free Corps will neither make war against Britain or the British Crown, nor support any action or policy detrimental to the interests of the British people.'

They insulted the intelligence of POWs by expecting us to believe this nonsense. The only result in our laager was one of ridicule and laughter. No one I questioned could name a single member of this so called 'corps'.

On September 17, five more POWs were killed while attempting to escape from one of our work camps. On the 26th, a bomb hit near our camp but there was no damage or injuries. Two days later, with hundreds of planes overhead, the town was hit again and the Jerrys took a work party of POWs from our camp to help dig up the dead and injured. Our Air Force was inflicting heavy damage on all of the major German cities, with reports of thousands being killed, and evacuees were pouring into Mühlhausen from the larger centres. Our work parties claimed that they were very hostile towards prisoners.

Another notice was posted on our bulletin board stating that, if escaping prisoners were caught in civilian clothing, they would be shot immediately as bandits, spies or saboteurs.

On November 25, we received the news that over 250 prisoners had been killed in a bombing raid on one of the work kommandos. We couldn't find out if it was a British or European camp. The air attacks were almost continuous and we spent more time in the shelters than above ground. In November, there was seldom a moment that heavy bombers with fighter escorts were not seen overhead and, on November 26, when I avoided going to the cellars by finding a new hiding place, I counted over 2,000 passing planes before tiring of the game and settling in to watch the constant dogfights.

The search for new hiding places during the raids continued. The dungeons were becoming unbearable. On December 1, our whole room of twelve men received twenty-one days strafe for not retreating to the shelters.

The camp at this time was alive with rumours. The latest one was that parachutists had been dropped in the area to act as fifth columnists. There was no doubt that the Allies were getting closer every day, and our main concern was to stay alive until they could reach us.

On December 14, we were ordered to draw the remainder of our Red Cross parcels from storage and were advised that there would be no more issues as Geneva was completely out of them. The bombing of depots and trains was again given as the reason. It looked like it was going to be a poor Christmas and a hungry winter!

Earlier that year, the camp had been cut off from receiving the German issue of coal briquettes, which were actually compressed coal dust. Each room had been getting three briquettes a day, not enough for warmth but at least enough to brew a tin can of water for tea. We had gradually burnt every piece of spare wood we could lay our hands on, including the bed slats that held our palliasse in place. It was a favourite sport to steal bed slats from other rooms and there was always a laugh at night when an unlucky prisoner whose bunk had been left with only two or three slats collapsed onto the man underneath. It wasn't so funny when you did the collapsing.

To offset this shortage, a wood party was formed to go out two or three times a week to dig up stumps from a forest about four kilometres from the camp. During these trips we were on an honour system not to escape as the wood was for our own benefit, even though the Germans used to insist on having two or three stumps from the load of about twenty that we gathered per trip. We had the use of an old sway-backed horse and a dilapidated four-wheeled wagon. The horse could handle the empty wagon but we had to help him with a full load. The poor creature didn't last long. He died on us, leaving us to do our own hauling. This was accomplished with the use of long ropes and about twelve to fifteen men.

One day, when we reached the wood we were surprised to see that the surrounding evergreens had the appearance of decorated Christmas trees, with silver strips glistening in the reflected sunlight. It was some time before we learned from a new Air Force prisoner that tin foil was being dropped to interfere with the use of German radar in spotting and locating Allied planes.

We welcomed the trips, which were more of a pleasure than a hardship, and we knew that escapes would be foolhardy, what with

"REMEMBER THE WOOD PARTYS"

SQUADRON SGT. MAJOR SIMPSON (CAMP LEADER
COMPANY " " WALLACE
" " " BROWN · M.M.
COY. QUARTER MASTER SGT. ROBERTSON.
" " " " FERGUSON
STAFF SGT. HEATON
LANCE SGT. VAN DE LEAR
SGT. JACK HINTON V.C.
SGTS. MCKAY · GABENAWAY · SKYRME
" DUNN · ROBERTS · CHRISTIE
" HUDSON · HEATH · SAVAGE
" MCLAINE
HALF SGT. BRALEY · GLIDER PILOT

CPL. PROUSE I/C
  - LISSON
  " ISBISTER
  - BRIGGS
  · BOSHOFF
  - LATERSON
  - COPELAND
  · BRUCE
  - SAMBRIDGE
GUNNER SHOREY
PTES. MALKIE · PRETORIAS

Note - when in 1944/5 we received no wood issue & practically no coal issue for our kitchens, heating, washing & showers etc. Partys pulled a cart to the woods everyday (horse died) a distance of approx. 3 miles uphill, for tree stumps which we dug out of clearing.

AND THE "PETER HOF" & "WELDFRIEDEN"

Men detailed to the wood party had some advantages, the best being a ration of canned jellied horsemeat from Argentina.

To boil water for a cup of tea was always a painstaking process, especially when fuel consisted mainly of wood shavings.

the Allied advance and constant bombing, plus the increasing itchiness of the Jerrys' gun fingers. The trips meant being away from the camp for the better part of a day, out in the fresh air and open surroundings of the forest. Another bonus was that the work party received an extra ration of bread and a tin of jellied horse meat to be shared between three men. This was the first meat that the Germans had given us and it had one of the sweetest and tenderest tastes that I had ever sampled. We learned later from one of the guards that the meat came from Argentina for the German army and was part of their rations until a number of them became sick from food poisoning. After a couple of them died, the tins were condemned for army consumption and in some mysterious manner had turned up at our camp. This was their loss and our gain, as not one of us had any problems.

The best part of the trip was the noon break, when the guards wanted to eat their lunch and have a beer in nearby Peterhof, a guest house (roadside pub). They couldn't leave us unguarded, so they would take us in the back door, where we had the use of a separate room and were able to buy beer by bribing the guards with Canadian cigarettes.

The woman innkeeper, who was fat and motherly, soon became used to us and we were able to trade with her now and then the usual Red Cross cocoa for brown bread. We asked her for eggs, having noticed some chickens out back. This she refused, evidently because they were too scarce. On one of our trips, on a visit to the washroom I climbed out of the window and managed to swipe two eggs from the hen house. That night each man in our combine of four had half an egg, a real trip to heaven and better than an orgasm. The others clustered around, having to be content with the smell of the frying eggs.

On December 25, 1944, we celebrated our third Christmas as POWs. On the 27th one of the boys was found dead in his bunk, a hell of an ending for a soldier! He was one of the Dunkirk men, and after so long in captivity his heart had finally failed.

By December 31, I had noted 115 raids for the month and on January 1, 1945, the sirens wailed again to start the New Year off on the right foot. The month of January gave us some respite from the cellars, as the alarm only sounded seventy-two times. We wondered if the bombing slowdown had any meaning, but the heavy raids started again in February.

It was remarkable how the prisoners stood up to the constant fear of being killed by a direct hit. Nerves were on edge, what with the lack of sleep and food and the many hours spent in the cellars, but morale in general was excellent. There were some who trembled visibly and had the wind up, but they were actually very few considering the large number of men in camp. No one ridiculed or blamed these men. Most went out of their way to talk with them and to sympathize, trying to get their minds away from the growing thoughts of impending doom.

Death was all around us. Another direct hit was scored on the town of Mühlhausen and nearby Gotha was heavily damaged with over four hundred killed, including eleven more POWs.

We continued our wood parties. One morning, on our way to the forest, we passed hundreds of evacuees fleeing from the larger cities. Most of them ignored us; a few glared in open hostility. Two or three spat at us as we passed and we were glad to reach the woods and the feeling of safety in its surroundings. During the morning, I dodged the guards and slipped deeper into the woods. I made a huge circle and came to the edge of the road where I watched for a German civilian whom I had approached on a previous trip. He had been gathering wood and I had asked if he wanted to trade bread for cocoa. He had agreed but seemed very nervous and I wasn't too sure if he would turn up. I couldn't be away from the wood party too long and was ready to give up when he came into sight. I whistled from the woods but he passed by without looking. I had to follow him for almost half a mile before he would venture into the woods. We quickly traded and he told me how scared he was of being caught. I got two loaves of bread for a tin of cocoa and stuffed them up the back of my tunic. I asked him to trade again on a future trip, but he was too frightened and scurried off.

I finally got back to the group and one of the guards spotted me entering the clearing. He shouted, wanting to know where I had been. I told him that I had had to take a crap and had felt sick, then offered him a cigarette to cool him down. He accepted and told me to get back to work. I rejoined the gang, who knew what I had been doing and had tried to cover for me.

On the return trip, my luck continued. I was the first to spot a large Belgian hare that had been run over and squashed flat by a truck. I scooped it up and hid it in a burlap bag of twigs that we used for starting the fires. That night, we threw the whole carcass into a pot, after cutting off the head, then boiled it with potatoes. We strained the fur out and the end results were excellent, making a soup that had grease bubbles with the distinct taste of meat.

During February, there was no respite from the bombing and the planes were now flying so low that we could read the markings. We learned that Arnstadt, Weimar and Jena were all heavily damaged and we could hear the crash of bombs much more distinctly than previously. There were more dogfights accompanied by the staccato sound of machine-gun fire and more planes were crashing in the area.

The attacks appeared to be centred on the area of Thuringen and, on our trips to the woods, we learned that the coal and gas supply to civilians had been cut off. On each trip we saw more and more civilians gathering wood and twigs.

On February 16, martial law was declared and it appeared that Germany was being bombed to its knees. The feeling in camp was one of excitement and elation, knowing that the end wasn't too far away. This feeling was heightened as more and more people were seen on the march. There was a continuous stream passing our building, including prisoners on the march from Poland and eastern Germany, as the Germans fell back from the Russian advance.

The sick prisoners, unable to march further, were dropped off at our already overcrowded camp. They were in very poor condition, suffering from dysentery and malnutrition, and they reminded me of the Russians we had seen at Stalag VIG. Trucks arrived daily with men who had dropped out of the march. In some cases, they were piled like cordwood with the bottom layers being dead. The camp doctor and medics did their best with the meagre supplies available but, for many, it had been their last trip. The German papers claimed that many of the marching prisoners had been killed by machine-gun fire from Russian planes.

On March 3, 1945, a notice was posted that read:

'TAKE YOUR CHOICE

If Germany collapses she will become Bolshevik. Other countries of the continent are on the way to becoming Soviet Republics. England will find herself isolated against a Soviet Europe and a Soviet Asia, from the Atlantic to the Pacific. This will be the end of your empire.

— — — — — — — — — —

Only a union of all European nations and their common co-operation with the British Empire can safeguard the existence of Europe, of her tradition and her civilization against an aggression from Siberia.

The very existence of the empire will then be secured and a permanent peace will be guaranteed for our continent after a long period of bloody fratricidal wars.

The present war consequently will be the last European conflict. _ _ _ _ _ _ _ _ _ _ _ _

Soldiers of all European countries are fighting for this aim united in the "European British Peace League".'

This, to us, was along the same lines as the call to join the 'British Free Corps'. The Jerrys would supply you with a German uniform, with a Union Jack on the sleeve and a 'British Free Corps' shoulder patch. All you had to do was volunteer to fight the Russians! They should have known better than to make such an offer. On a previous occasion, when they had learned how well the German prisoners were treated in Canada, they had posted a notice offering all Canadian prisoners a chance to move to a separate and better camp for the use of Canadians only. This offer was turned down flatly by the senior Canadian representative and the Germans were advised that we were all one and the same and, if the whole camp was not included, we didn't want any part of it.

Another offer made periodically was a trip to Berlin for any prisoner who agreed to speak on the radio, telling the folks back home how well we were treated. Unfortunately, some men did take advantage of this, just to ease the monotony of prison life. They were very few in number and were marked men from then on.

On March 5, Weimar was bombed and sixty prisoners were killed out of the thousands on the march. Our camp, which normally held 500 men, had swollen to more than 1,000 with additional prisoners arriving daily. Twelve more arrived on that day, the survivors of a group that started out with forty-two. Thirty of them died on the march, some from dysentery and others from the machine-gunning planes.

On March 7, medics were sent from our camp to the nearby woods to retrieve the bodies of seven airmen shot down in dogfights. It was sad to see men cut down in the prime of their lives but we couldn't dwell too long on these happenings and keep our sanity. Death was becoming a daily affair and each man fought for his own survival. The only good news of the day was that Dresden had been flattened.

On March 14, the camp was completely out of wood. Once

again, fifteen of us left for the usual trip to the woods for stumps. On our return, the guards came out to take their share. The whole load consisted of around twenty stumps, which were loaded with the larger ones on the bottom of the high-sided wagon. The roots were all interlocked, making it difficult to unload. This was planned in advance with the idea of letting the Jerrys have only the small stumps on the top of the load. This time our plan backfired as an *unter offizier* (equivalent of a sergeant) supervised the operation and had the guards unload the whole wagon. He grabbed the three largest stumps and this started an argument, as there were far more prisoners waiting for wood than Jerry guards. I got involved in a heated argument with one officer and we stood nose to nose in a shouting match. I thought I was getting the best of the argument (I had a larger nose) but he was outdoing me in the screaming department and finally pulled his pistol from its holster and started waving it in my face.

The noise of the argument brought the confidant man out of the camp and he quickly stepped between us, telling me to cool it as the Jerry was threatening to shoot me. This made me all the more angry and I dared the bastard to pull the trigger, shouting that I'd kill him before I went down. I don't know what the outcome would have been if the Commandant hadn't come on the scene and called us all to attention. He literally screamed at the officer to put his gun away and ordered the guards to put us inside the camp. I guess I lost the argument—they wound up with the three largest stumps.

The following day, we watched from the cell windows as thousands of prisoners marched past us in flight from the eastern camps. They had to leave almost two hundred in the town of Mühlhausen who could no longer continue the march. Ten of the worst cases were brought to our overcrowded camp and several of these were dead the next day.

On the 19th, we received anti-typhus injections. Lice were now in the camp, brought in by the daily arrivals. On the 21st there was a further cut in the German rations. We now received a two-kilo loaf of bread between nine men per day. On the 22nd, we had a burial for fourteen men. Some were airmen who had been shot down, the rest were prisoners who came in off the march. On this same day we could hear the sound of big guns in the distance. This gave us a much needed lift and we were further encouraged by the underground news that the Allies had crossed the Rhine. This meant that the Western front was only 200 kilometres away. We had already heard that the Russians on the Eastern front were 300 kilometres away from us.

On the following day, while on our usual wood party, the wagon got away from us on the return trip and two of the gang got broken toes as the wheels passed over their feet. On the 26th we received our second anti-typhus injection. But the big news arrived on March 20 in the form of two POW officers who had marched in a column from Rotenburg. They told us that an Allied spearhead had reached Kassel, only 90 kilometres from our camp. The following morning, the Germans took a large number of prisoners out of the camp on a work party. On their return, we learned that they had been forced to erect road blocks and dig tank traps on the road leading into Mühlhausen.

On March 31, our wood party was cancelled because of the large number of bomber and fighter planes overhead. At 4:30 p.m., as we watched from our cell windows, the planes attacked to the east of the town in the direction of the forest where we usually got our stumps. We figured that the Jerry soldiers had taken cover there. The attack was then centred on the town, where a large German barracks was situated. As night fell, red flares were seen overhead and the sound of machine-gun fire was almost constant. We didn't get too much sleep that night, listening to the attack and wondering how far the Allies had to go to reach us.

On Easter Sunday, April 1, the air raids subsided. We were getting ready to go to the forest as we desperately needed wood, if not for heat, at least for cooking. Before I began to dress, I indulged my constant habit of jotting down notes and then hiding them for future use. In so doing, I realized that this past month had been the worst for air raids so far, with a total of 179 alarms lasting 235 hours. The longest alert in one day was $16\frac{1}{2}$ hours. No wonder we were getting 'bomb happy'!

When we were finally ready to go, I noticed that the Jerrys sent more guards than usual with us. We soon found out why. There were endless streams of civilians, evacuees from bombed cities, carrying bundles and suitcases and in some cases pushing prams and other wheeled vehicles containing their worldly belongings. Along the sides of the roads were burned-out German tanks, scout cars and trucks, victims of the constant air raids. As we passed along the edge of the forest, we became aware that the woods were alive with Jerry troops. One of the guards left us to talk to a German officer who stood by the side of the road. When he returned, we heard him telling the other guards that the area was completely surrounded by the Allies and that the other officer had warned him against proceeding any further. The guards halted us, discussed the situation among themselves and then decided to go ahead to our usual stump gathering area, as per their orders.

We had just started digging, when all hell broke loose overhead. One minute the sky was clear and the next it was full of diving and swooping planes locked in a deadly air fight. All the men hit the ground and slowly turned over with faces up to watch the fight. Every plane seemed to have another one on its tail, and the action was so fast we couldn't tell which belonged to us or the Jerrys. Some planes dived so low in trying to shake off their pursuers that they couldn't come out of the dive and crashed into the ground with a thunderous roar. Others were shot down and crashed in flames, setting the surrounding trees ablaze. The machine-gun fire was constant and, when all of a sudden the fighting was over, the silence seemed strange and eerie.

Slowly we picked ourselves up. It seemed that everyone wanted to talk at once. There was nervous laughter and then the work proceeded once again as the guards yelled at us to get the job finished as quickly as possible. When we had the wagon half loaded, we suddenly noticed that there were German troops all around us and that our guards were arguing and shouting at them. The air was very hostile and our guards told us that half a wagon was enough. They were having increasing difficulty in keeping the troops from attacking us and had decided to cut the trip short and get back to camp. What with the angry glares and menacing gestures from the Jerry troops, we agreed with the guards completely and only breathed easy when we got back on the road.

We could understand the anger of the German troopers, what with the constant bombing and the knowledge that they were in full retreat. It was only natural that when they saw the uniform of their enemy, they didn't see khaki, they saw red. We were glad to get back to camp and its temporary safety and to hear the latest news. We were told that a British and French POW camp, taken by the Russians and then recaptured by the Germans, was found with all prisoners murdered, presumably by the Russians. We believed this to be German propaganda and wrote it off as such. We also learned that typhus had broken out in the main camp of Stalag IXC in Bad Sulza.

The heavy raids continued during the night and in the distance we could see the glow of flames lighting up the sky over Eisenach. The sound of guns was getting closer and we finally fell into a

Soon after capture, we thought the war would never end. But as bombing raids increased and refugees criss-crossed the countryside, we knew liberation was near.

troubled sleep. At 2:00 a.m., on April 2, we were rudely awakened and told to prepare for evacuation. We packed our kits with the little food we had left and scrounged around for water bottles.

At 8:00 a.m. we left the sick and disabled prisoners behind and marched out of the camp for the last time.

9: Forced March to Liberation

COMMUNAL DECLARATION MADE BY THE BRITISH, BELGIAN, FRENCH, RUSSIAN AND SERB MEN OF CONFIDENCE

The Camp, being in isolation for a period of 21 days, has not been called upon to evacuate. The German Command has been taken over by Hauptmann Lehr assisted by a reduced staff, and the British, Belgian, French, Russian and Serb Men of Confidence have decided, by common agreement, in the present exceptional period, to take - after having referred to the officers of the different nationalities in the camp - the direction of the camp in order to avoid any incidents prejudicial to us all.

Each prisoner must understand that he is and remains above everything else a soldier, under military discipline which in no case will be neglected.

Consequently:

1) No act of pillage will be tolerated, so that material, fuel and provisions may be used to the advantage of all;

2) No personal repression will be exercised;

3) No one will be allowed to leave the camp, except on Red Cross and ration fatigues, and in exceptional cases, with a pass given with our agreement;

4) Barracks and Billets must be kept clean. Fatigue parties will be formed for this purpose.

We have decided to create, in order to lighten our task, a Provost Section under the command of the French Sergeant-Major LAURANT, assisted:

- for the British	by	T.S.M. DERRY
- for the Belgians	by	HAUSTRATE
- for the Russians	by	DEMCHENKO
- for the Serbs	by	MILOCHEVITCH

They will be helped by a party of men to be chosen by themselves, and they will all wear a special arm-band.

Those responsible for the various camp services (interpreter, barrack chiefs, group leaders, kitchen, baths, M.I. Room, etc...) will continue as in the past to carry out their duties in the interest of the camp and under our authority.

Finally, the orders are as follows, and are the instructions received from the Allies:

Stay grouped inside the camp and keep the greatest calm.

While waiting for the arrival in the camp of the Allies, the British, Belgian, French, Russian and Serb Men of Confidence specially ask their comrades to show patience, discipline, and good will and the widest understanding of the grave problems to be solved whilst awaiting definite liberation

BAD SULZA, the 11th April 1945

The last notice posted before liberation.

CHAPTER 9

Forced March to Liberation

On the first day we marched twenty-one kilometres, joining thousands of other prisoners clogging the roads, and eventually arrived on the outskirts of Ebenleben. We were herded into barns and sank gratefully into the sweet-smelling hay for a night's rest.

We awoke cold and stiff from the unaccustomed marching and again took to the roads. We were constantly on the alert for diving planes that were machine-gunning all moving vehicles, freight trains and railway depots. In the early evening, we arrived at Hottenhausen, after foot slogging for another twenty-six kilometres. By this time we realized what poor condition we were in. We nursed our blistered feet and tried to forget the soreness in our shoulders caused by the heavy packs. We were glad to bed down that night, again in barns and outbuildings.

On April 4, we had only marched a few kilometres when some men began dumping their belongings to lighten the load. I dumped everything I considered unnecessary, keeping only a blanket, mess tin and the little food I had left. I couldn't bring myself to discard my notes and diary, so I stuffed these inside my tunic, along with a dog-eared copy of *The Robe*. I had waited almost a year to get this book and was damned if I was going to toss it away without finishing it. I managed to read it while marching and found it took my mind off the aches and pains.

We travelled twenty-seven kilometres that day to another small town called Grossneuhausen and once again holed up in a barn. Despite my fatigue, I had difficulty sleeping. There was a constant dull ache in my stomach, my shoulders and feet were sore and my knees had started to act up. What a hell of a condition to be in at a time like this!

As I lay there, listening to the snores of men and the squealing of mice, my thoughts returned to England. I wondered who was riding my motorbike. It seemed crazy to dwell on such a subject, but anyone who's ridden a bike for two years, eaten on it and slept on it, will understand how a person can miss it. I forgot all about being wet and cold and the aggravation of motorcycle breakdowns. I'd even have forgotten my three major spills if it hadn't been for the ache in my knees caused by torn cartilages following one of the upsets. The dull ache in my gut was also a reminder, as it

German civilian ration coupons were 'liberated' from a vacant house as
our search for food got underway.

had first occurred after the initial year of bike riding. But I turned my mind back to the good times and fell soundly asleep to the roar of the motorcycle and the sound of the wind as I sped off into nowhere.

On April 5 (the same day, we later learned, that Mühlhausen was liberated by the Americans), we marched to the outskirts of Sommerda. The column was halted as the town was under air attack. We watched as factories were demolished by the falling bombs and had a front-line seat for the ensuing air battle between the fighter planes of the opposing sides. The Germans were out-classed. Soon their fighters were falling in flames or breaking off the fight and disappearing in the clouds.

The Allied planes were in control and, as we resumed the march, they dived low over the column trying to identify friend or foe. Unfortunately for us, German troops had infiltrated our column to escape the devastating machine-gun attacks. The Allied planes must have become aware of this as one squadron after the other peeled off and headed for the column with machine guns roaring. There was a mad scramble as both prisoners and Germans hit the ditches or raced for the fields to escape the rain of destruction. One senior NCO, remembering the instructions that had filtered though to us from Intelligence, quickly laid two long strips of white cloth side by side, a signal meaning 'POWs in danger'. The attack was broken off and an audible sigh of relief was heard. The column marched off, leaving some men, both prisoners and Germans, beyond caring for.

As we passed through Sommerda, we could see the *Volk Sturm* (People's Army) digging at the rubble of bombed buildings and erecting barricades against the advancing Allies.

With the diving planes and constant halts, we only marched eighteen kilometres to Herrengosserstadt that day. En route, the air activity was still deadly. We were constantly hitting the dirt. We saw a direct hit on a moving train and watched the planes devastate another railway depot. It was like watching a first-class war movie.

There were literally thousands of people on the roads, a mixture of British, French, Polish and Russian prisoners, plus German troops and fleeing civilians. It was a mad beehive of activity, and I felt certain that our guards had orders to march us in circles to avoid having us freed by the advancing British, Canadians and Americans on one side and the Russian army on the other. The whole scene reminded me of an ant hill that had been disturbed, with each ant dashing madly in circles, trying to get back to its home and security.

We encamped in farm fields that night and, before we could get bedded down, hundreds of Polish women prisoners were marched into the next field, separated from us only by barbed wire and the large man-like Nazi women guards armed with huge wooden batons which they wielded freely. There was a mad dash for the fence as both sides tried to communicate. They were in pitiful condition, with their clothes in rags and their feet clad in burlap sacks. They clamoured for food, cigarettes and soap and kept repeating the word 'Jig-a-Jig', which we had come to recognize as an international meaning for sex. We tried to throw things to them, a little of what we had left, but the huge women guards beat them back unmercifully and our guards moved in on us.

On April 6, the guards decided to keep us in the same location for another day and night as some of the prisoners were in very poor condition and unfit for marching. I lay awake until about 2:00 a.m., too hungry to sleep, and finally decided to take a chance and go in search of food. I had noticed a small cluster of houses about half a mile from the field; when we had marched past the day before a group of women had waved to the column in a friendly manner.

The time seemed endless as I worked my way through the fields flat on my stomach. I finally reached the perimeter marked only by four strands of barbed wire. The guards on duty were strung out along the wire but there were long gaps between them. I was in a cold sweat as I eased my way under the bottom strand and for a moment felt fear and almost gave up. My growling stomach dictated otherwise, and with one last roll I was under the wire and into the roadside ditch.

Fortunately the ditch was deep and almost water-free. I was able to crawl on all fours until I was well clear of the camp. It didn't take me too long to reach the cluster of houses I had seen, but it did take me endless minutes to make up my mind which house to approach. I almost chickened out, picturing the occupants screaming for help and guards rushing from every direction to shoot me down. It was a stupid and thoughtless plan, but with my nature I knew I had to go through with it.

I circled the house I had chosen and tapped gently on the back door. Nothing happened and I repeated the tapping, almost wishing no one would hear and I could get the hell out of there. I was about ready to give up when I saw the light from a candle. The door opened slightly and a woman's voice asked me in German what I wanted. I told her that I was a prisoner-of-war and wanted food in exchange for some soap, cigarettes and a tin of cocoa. She told me that she was a Polish field worker and that these houses were occupied by a group of Polish women prisoners who worked the farm for the Germans. She asked me to wait a minute and seemed very nervous. She finally came back to the door and handed me a loaf of bread and a small cabbage. I gave her a bar of soap, half a deck of cigarettes and almost a full tin of cocoa. She wished me luck and I took off, cramming the bread and cabbage up the back of my tunic and tightening my belt.

I made my way back to the ditch, crawled the length of it until I was back to the camp and gingerly raised my head to see how the land lay. I almost let out a yell as I saw one of the guards patrolling the fence in front of me. I quickly ducked down and almost exploded trying to hold my breath. When I got up enough courage to take another look, he was about fifty of sixty yards away. I looked in the other direction. Another guard was still further down the fence. I quickly scrambled under the wire and squirmed back to my blanket and safety.

I had to awaken a couple of the boys to brag about the night's adventure and share the grub. They weren't interested in how or where I had obtained the food, but only in getting something to fill the void in their stomachs. It wasn't a gourmet meal, but when you're hungry any food is like manna from heaven. We finally fell asleep with a satisfied sigh.

When I was out of the camp, I had thought of how easy it would be to escape. I had no idea of where the Allied lines were, however, and, with the large numbers of hostile troops and civilians around, I felt it was foolhardy at this stage of the game to take any unnecessary chances. From all the signs around us, including the frantic actions of the Germans, it wouldn't be too much longer before we were freed. The main thing now was to stay alive until that moment arrived.

On April 7, the guards decided to move us and we were on the march again. Before the day was over, men started to throw up, complaining of violent gut aches and diarrhoea. We had been drinking ditch water and eating anything we could get our hands on. This, no doubt, was the cause of the problem.

I was all right until early evening and then it hit me like a sledge hammer. It felt as if a giant fist had pounded into my stomach. I started to vomit and couldn't control my bowels. I kept having to drop out of the column with others as the guards yelled and prodded us with the butts of their rifles. All I wanted to do was lay down and die and to hell with the guards, but they thought otherwise. It was an unending cycle: run to the side of the road, throw up, go, be prodded back to the column and repeat the action over and over again. The only thing I was thankful for was my copy of *The Robe*, which provided the only toilet paper I had. It was a great book in more ways than one!

When the march was finally halted the men fell into the hay in utter exhaustion. There wasn't much sleep that night, as we kept stumbling out of the barn retching and heaving, only to return to the terrible stench of men too weak to move who were lying in their own filth. I kept wondering how low we must sink before this rotten ordeal would be over.

In the morning, I staggered out of the barn, glad to get into the fresh air and away from the horrible scene within. I looked around for some place to go. There was no privacy and nothing but a large pile of cow and horse manure in the centre of the courtyard. This was surrounded by squatting men with the spaces shared by pecking hens, pigeons and ducks. We gave and they received. I awaited my turn around the pile, desperately trying to hold on. I finally got a place and, as I glanced upwards, I noticed two German peasant women leaning out of the windows, gossiping and completely ignoring the misery that was enacted beneath them.

The guards routed us out and we marched another eighteen kilometres to Schmiedehausen. On the way, many men gave up, too sick and weak to march any further. The guards finally gave up trying to prod them to their feet and left them where they lay, either to die or make it later on their own.

Planes were bombing and strafing all day, but we were too sick to care what anyone was doing. All the men just wanted to lie down and be left alone. We knew the end must be near, as all we had been doing was walking in circles. The Germans knew they had been beaten but seemed afraid to surrender. There were pockets of resistance where the Nazi party kept villagers fighting on, hoping against hope for a miracle that would turn the tide of battle. What a hope! I simply couldn't understand why they didn't just leave, let the people surrender and get us the hell out of there.

We continued to march with difficulty, constantly falling behind the column to relieve ourselves. With this form of dysentery, we would no sooner get back to the column than we would have to fall out again. Rear guards kept prodding us but we were so sick and weak that we simply ignored their shouts and threats.

Towards evening, the worst cases, myself among them, were cut out of the column and marched a painfully slow five kilometres to Bad Sulza, the main camp of Stalag IXC. The camp doctor and the medics worked overtime to help deal with the new arrivals, and with their limited medical supplies they somehow worked wonders.

I'll always be grateful to the Scottish medic who stood me up, held a fist in my stomach and with his free hand held the back of my neck and forced my head between my knees. He repeated this action three times, and when he straightened me up he told me to shove my finger down my throat. Whatever his method, it sure worked. I threw up violently and couldn't seem to stop until I felt completely empty. This same man then gave me two large spoonfuls of dry cocoa and a small square of cheese. He laid me down and covered me with a blanket and I immediately fell into an exhausted sleep.

When I finally awoke, I felt like a new man. The runs had stopped and the only signs of my illness were a feeling of weakness and a very sore rear end. This was nothing compared to some men who had piles the size of chicken eggs.

In the afternoon, I was able to get into the courtyard and take stock of my new surroundings. It was a much larger camp than Molsdorf or Mühlhausen and contained prisoners of many nationalities. The different groups were separated only by barbed wire fences. The large group 'next door' were Russians in their dark green uniforms. These prisoners looked haggard and hungry and held a look of desperation in their eyes. Whenever I sighted these men, I always felt sorry for them. Their plight seemed much more desperate than ours. I had landed at Dieppe weighing between 175 and 180 pounds. During my term as a prisoner, I had dropped to 160 pounds. After the long march and the dysentery, I was 130 pounds soaking wet and still felt fat beside the Russian prisoners.

That night there was a continuous drone in the sky as planes bombed Jena and Apolda. At times it was almost as bright as day, with the many flares hanging in the sky and the searchlights stabbing and probing the upper darkness. The constant sound of ack-ack fire was only interrupted by the heavy crash of bombs that shook the buildings and had the ground continuously trembling as if in fear.

Right : The first German officer to surrender to me was quick to show me snapshots.

Below : It was a delicious feeling to be the jailors instead of the jailed. A group photo of our first batch of prisoners.

More of our friends arrived in the camp, cut out of the march which was now apparently headed for Hof in Saxony. We were supposed to be moved to the hospital in Stadtroda in groups of twenty-four, but at the last minute the move was cancelled since we would have had to pass through Jena which was still under air attack.

On April 10, not only the bombing continued but planes began diving and machine-gunning too close to our camp for comfort. Two freight trains on tracks alongside our camp were strafed with machine-gun fire and the empty shell casings fell into our enclosure. We were all flat on our faces praying for survival when suddenly I remembered what had been done with two white strips of cloth on the march. I worked my way to one of the buildings, entered what appeared to be a deserted officers' room and grabbed a white sheet from the bed. Climbing to the roof of the building, I had just started to tear the sheet in half when I heard the familiar roar of approaching fighters. Glancing upwards, I could see the approaching squadron and, before I could put my intention into action, one of the planes peeled off and started his dive. I waved the sheet frantically as the plane came in at roof level. I swear he was so low that I expected to be cut down with a burst from his gun or at least hit and swept off the building. Instead, he dipped his wing at the last minute, zoomed upwards, and rejoined the squadron.

My trembling knees buckled and I sat down hard on the roof unable to move for several minutes. Before I climbed down, I watched as plane after plane dived on adjacent buildings with machine-guns chattering in a staccato melody of death and destruction.

German fighters appeared and the inevitable dogfights commenced. Planes dropped with black smoke trailing and parachutists billowed through the sky as the flyers tried to escape. Where Allied flyers were floating down, their comrades circled them to prevent them from being cut down by German fighters still in the area.

In the early hours of dawn, one of the guards told us that the front was only eight kilometres away. We could easily believe this, not only from the air action but from the sound of heavy shell fire gradually getting closer and closer. It was a scary feeling, being in the middle of the battle, but at the same time it was exciting and exhilarating to think of impending freedom.

There was a sudden commotion in the Russian enclosure next

to ours. As we watched helplessly, the Jerry guards rushed in with fixed bayonets and started to prod the prisoners toward the gates in an obvious attempt to evacuate the camp and keep them out of the hands of the approaching Allies. There was a lot of screaming and shouting as the Russians tried to hang back and elude the prodding guards. Finally, shooting broke out and the camp was quickly emptied except for the dead and wounded laying in the courtyard.

Our turn came next. A large group of Germans entered our enclosure. They commenced the same procedure of prodding and shouting at us to move out. Not a man moved. The whole camp was determined that this was it: freedom was too near. The officer in charge of the guards screamed that either we moved out or we would be shot. The prisoners held their ground and glared in defiance. For a moment there was an ominous silence, suddenly broken by the unmistakable sound of approaching tanks. We knew this was our salvation and let out a thunderous cheer. The Jerrys took to their heels, rushing out of the main gate and disappearing in full flight.

At 5:05 p.m. on April 11, the tanks of the American Third Army arrived at the gates of the camp. We rushed out to greet them and they showered us with cigarettes and field rations. One trooper even stripped off his battle jacket and handed it to me, no doubt feeling sorry for my ragged appearance. The officer in charge laid out a map, asking directions and locations of other POW camps. We pointed these out and also gave them the general map location of our still marching comrades. Before they left, we told them the direction that the fleeing guards had taken and asked them to give them hell.

The tanks of Patton's Army moved out with motors roaring and tracks grinding to continue their pursuit of the fleeing Germans. In short order we heard the sound of battle; they evidently met some resistance nearby. It didn't last long and the battle sounds faded into the distance.

We began rounding up Jerry prisoners in the immediate vicinity. For years I had dreamed of this moment of revenge but when I came face to face with the first Jerry to surrender to me, all I could feel was compassion as I saw the fear in his eyes and noticed his trembling lips and hands. I escorted him to our camp, where we had set up a temporary prisoner compound, and even handed him a cigarette and let him show me snaps of his wife and children. Why, oh, why couldn't my first prisoner have been 'Plank-face'?

Above and Overleaf: These personal snapshots were taken from our prisoners as souvenirs.

After the round-up, we received instructions from the military authorities to stay close to our camp for our own safety. This was sensible but, after almost three years of confinement and being as hungry as a bear I knew what I'd be doing first thing in the morning.

On April 12, I volunteered to do the scrounging for our combine and left the camp at first light for the town. I was constantly challenged by Belgian and French ex-prisoners wearing arm bands. They had been chosen to police the area in an effort to maintain law and order until the situation had stabilized. I identified myself and explained my mission and they allowed me to proceed after warning me to be careful of bands of Russians, Poles and Serbs who had armed themselves and were on the prowl, looting, drinking and firing their guns wildly at anything that moved.

I reached the town, which was bedecked with white flags flying from almost every building and window. I could hear sporadic firing as small pockets of resistance were cleared out and the shouts of roaming bands of ex-prisoners as they went wild in their newly obtained freedom.

I found a large house all boarded up, tore the boards from one of the windows and climbed through in the search for food. The large dining-room table was set with a hastily prepared meal which was only partly consumed. There were German uniforms on the beds and on the floors as if the occupants had shed their connection with the German army, eaten in haste and departed.

I ate my fill of German sausage and bread and then rummaged through the dresser drawers. I found snap shots of the former occupants; one of them was a high-ranking officer posing with Hitler. I took these and other pictures with Hitler in them as personal souvenirs and then went back to the dining room to load up with food for my buddies. When I had taken all the food available, I noticed a large jar of blueberry preserves on top of a sideboard. I put it to my lips and drank the sweet and heavenly juice, munching on the berries. I was in second heaven.

Suddenly, I heard a noise disturb the silence of the semi-darkened house. I yelled, 'Who's there?' This was answered by the sound of a shot, magnified in the close quarters. I heard the whistle of a bullet and instinctively tensed as it rushed past my head.

As a second shot rang out, I felt a thump in my stomach and could feel blood running down my front and legs. I staggered towards the window and tumbled to the ground. Slowly, I got to

The search for food in local houses turned up more souvenirs, despite the general prohibition against looting. The real prize from a *gauleiter*'s home was the snapshot of Hitler.

my feet, wondering at the lack of pain. In the early morning light I undid my trousers to look at the damage. The 'blood' was purple and turned out to be blueberry juice covering my front from the waist down. I chuckled in relief and then went helpless with laughter as I realized what had happened.

When the first shot rang out, I had lowered the jar from my lips. On the second shot, I had slammed the jar against my middle in a reflex action. Feeling the impact and the jar's contents spilling down my front, illusion was complete. Such is the power of imagination!

I got the hell out of there fast, not trying to figure out who had fired the shots and caring less. I felt lucky to be alive, even if I did have a purple penis.

I dropped the grub off at the camp and went looking for meat and vegetables. I had no trouble finding onions and potatoes, but couldn't turn up fresh meat until I came across the town depot. To the side of this building, there was a long row of wire cages, each holding a large Belgian hare, the largest I have ever seen. I picked up a piece of iron pipe, opened one of the cages, and tried to kill the animal. I met resistance, first from the hare, which was stronger than I thought, and then from the station master who came running from the station waving a shotgun, determined to protect his property. It was a stand-off until an American jeep came on the scene. When I told them my reason for wanting the hare, they fired a burst of machine-gun fire at the old fellow's feet. He dropped his gun and ran. They then turned the gun on the hares, killing three of them. I thanked the Yanks and made off with my prizes, returning to the camp in triumph. What a meal we had that night. The hare was cooked with onions and potatoes and carrots in a huge stew, our first 'real' meal in close to three years.

The next day I left the camp again, on the prowl for anything I could find. I ran into a French ex-prisoner who told me where large quantities of wine and champagne were stored. He led me to a huge concrete building with the Nazi emblem emblazoned across the front. It turned out to be where they stored wines looted from occupied countries such as France. Entering the building, we came across a wild celebration. Prisoners of all nations were breaking open cases, sampling the contents, then throwing the bottles aside until they found something more to their liking. I picked a case of champagne and lugged it back to the camp. On my way I ran into the two soldiers who had helped me get the hares the previous day. I repaid them by giving them directions for the fine wines.

On a second trip, with others from the camp to help carry more cases, we were out of luck. Someone had put a torch to the building and it was now engulfed in flames. Disappointed, we started to make our way back to the camp. En route, two or three stray German fighters dived on the now occupied town, spraying everything moving with machine-gun fire. We dashed for shelter behind an American tank as it opened up against the diving planes. Other guns quickly joined the action and one of the planes was soon hurtling earthward in flames as the others disappeared into the cloud cover.

Later that afternoon, I located the main records for Stalag IXC and, after much searching, found my personal records as a POW. (I already had my official photo which I had obtained from the hospital records when first captured.) I searched through the various huts. One contained nothing but POW photos, another was full of confiscated cameras, yet another had watches and lighters, etc. All buildings had been entered before. The last hut, which contained currency, was knee-deep in bills dumped from the various drawers. I took one bill from each country that I could find, then noticed stacks of new bills in their original wrappers piled in one corner of the room. They turned out to be 'Italian Occupation' currency used by the invading Allies. I took only one thin sheaf as a souvenir. (Later, on my return to England, I found that I was able to trade it for British currency through a Canadian officer who had been in the occupation forces in Italy. I kicked myself that I hadn't taken a kit bag full.)

My last sortie was in the late afternoon, when I entered the local town hall. This was full of prisoners looking for German Lugers. The hall was piled high with cast-off German uniforms, as if a whole company had changed here into civvies before fleeing. I kicked something hard as I sorted through the clothing and a Luger slithered across the floor. Other hands quickly snatched it up and I was denied the main souvenir I had been searching for. I had to be satisfied with a Jerry helmet, a dress bayonet, a field bayonet well notched with 'kills', plus assorted badges.

Returning to camp, I passed a German officer still in uniform, complete with the red Nazi arm band. He was being dragged along by two American soldiers who had routed him from his hiding place. I stopped to talk with them, saying that this was the type of German that should be shot. They claimed that he most likely would be and I said, 'He won't need this any longer,' and relieved him of his arm band.

At 2:00 p.m. on April 14, our third day of freedom, we were loaded into American supply trucks for evacuation and driven to the aerodrome in Langan Salza, which was found to be too heavily damaged for the landing of planes. It was decided to transport us to Gotha, where we found both the town and aerodrome in a tangled mess. The airstrip was found to be OK for landing, however, so we were left there to spend the night. The planes would not arrive until the following morning.

It was very cold and, as I had ditched my great-coat, I searched around for something warm to cover me for the night. I came across the body of a dead Jerry flyer still clad in his flying suit. Donning this, I found a sheltered corner in one of the partly demolished buildings and slept fitfully during my last night in Germany.

On April 15, we had a considerable wait before the planes arrived. In my wanderings I discovered a very large oil painting of Hitler hanging on the still-standing end wall of the main airport building. With the help of a very long ladder, I cut the painting from the frame and rolled it, as we had been told that we could take all the souvenirs we could carry on the plane. The painting was approximately twenty-to-twenty-four-feet high and fifteen-feet wide and, when the plane finally arrived, the pilot of the troop carrier said there was no way I could take it with me; the plane just wasn't long enough! Hitler may have died in his Berlin bunker but to me he died on the airstrip in Gotha.

We took off in the C-47 at 2:30 p.m. and, except for a two-hour refuelling stop at Rheims, flew directly over the Channel to England.

Epilogue

"IN THE LAND OF BEGIN AGAIN"

In this cartoon, copied from one appearing in *The Camp*, the smile on the soldier's face says everything there is to say about the dreams of a POW.

Epilogue

We landed at Westcott around 6:00 p.m. and were greeted by an air force band. We were quickly sprayed with delousing powder, handed cigarettes and treated to a light supper served by women of the WAAF. The highlight of the meal was the white bread, which, after our long diet of black bread, looked and tasted like cake. The same night, we were taken by truck to a reception camp at Wotton near Aylesbury, where we were washed, fed, issued with new uniforms and put to bed.

On April 16, we awoke to a beautiful breakfast of bacon and eggs, the thing I dreamt about in prison camp and missed the most. After breakfast, we had our medicals and X-rays, then lined up for pay parade. On the 17th, we were trucked to Aylesbury, then to London, then to No. 1 Canadian Reception Depot in, of all places, Aldershot!

In passing through London, I recalled the 'Battle of Britain' and the terrible bomb damage. It seemed even worse now from the effect of the V-Bombs. (A V-Bomb depot was later discovered in Nordhausen, one of our work kommandos in Stalag IXC. Mass graves were also found there.)

In Aldershot, two of my former Provost buddies arrived to cart me off for wining and dining. One was now a major, later to become lieutenant colonel, and the other a captain. I felt a twinge of jealousy, being only a corporal but, after a few drinks and a lot of reminiscing, rank was forgotten. I actually began to feel enriched by the POW experience.

The following day, I was sent to London for interrogation about treatment, beatings, my two escapes and any known collaborators. Finally, I was photographed and finger-printed, then returned to Aldershot.

We were allowed any number of passes for leave but I delayed my trips until I could regain some of the fifty pounds I had lost in weight. I wasn't too proud of my appearance and wanted to lose the gaunt look and fill out some of the hollow spots before visiting friends and sightseeing. Eventually, I took advantage of the passes to revisit many spots on the south coast such as Brighton, Bournemouth and Eastbourne, not to mention many trips to London.

In London, all an ex-POW had to do was to show his dog tags

and he received 1,000 Canadian cigarettes and a forty-pound food parcel from Canada House, a service man's club. I took my second parcel to relatives in Birmingham, as they were still on war ration coupons which weren't much good.

My first parcel barely made it past Trafalgar Square. A buddy and I shouldered our food cartons and headed for the station, but before we could reach it, we were hustled by street characters wanting to know if we had anything to sell. We finally gave in and opened the cartons full of canned fruits, meats and vegetables. We finished selling everything and then returned to Canada House for another parcel. They were very understanding and obliged us since we were former prisoners but they told us not to come back a third time.

After visiting the relatives in bombed-out Birmingham, my next trip was to Scotland to say adieu to my escape buddy and relive our experiences over a few drinks. Oddly, Tommy and I weren't too voluble. We had shared a harrowing chapter of our lives but now we respected each other's feelings and need for privacy.

On the return trip, I ran into another ex-POW who asked me what 'loot' I had brought out of Germany. When I told him of the badges, tin hat and Hitler snap shots he laughed and said, 'I mean this kind of loot'. He then unknotted a handkerchief and showed me a small heap of diamonds which just about dazzled me. I had passed boarded-up jewellery stores after release but it hadn't entered my head to go in and 'acquire' some of the contents. Maybe it was just as well.

During the train ride back to barracks, I found an empty compartment, stretched out and fell asleep immediately. My sleep was troubled with dreams of massive air raids as I dodged and ducked falling bombs. This was followed by a Jerry lunging at me with his fixed bayonet. As I was unarmed, I tried to kick the rifle from his hands. He dropped it and grabbed the heel and toe of my heavy army boot. At this moment, I awakened to find an English soldier and his girl friend, who had entered the compartment while I slept, strugging to hold my lashing foot as I tried to kick their teeth out! I was embarrassed and apologized. The soldier's only comment was, 'It's OK, Canada. I have those kind of dreams also.' This helped but I still felt foolish and changed compartments.

My last trip was to London on May 8. It was 'VE Day' and I'll never forget the wild celebration in Piccadilly Circus. The pandemonium was a fitting end to almost six years of war. I personally had a feeling of thankfulness that I had come through OK and, apart from some injuries, was relatively healthy. I was beginning to regain my weight and had lost that starved look. The main feeling I had was of being free, free to come and go wherever I wanted. The other important part of freedom was being able to buy food and drink; the glorious feeling of waking up to a meal of bacon and eggs, toast and hot coffee; the absolute thrill of a dish of vanilla ice cream; the wonder of white bread.

On May 29, we entrained for Liverpool and embarked on the *SS Vollendam*, which apart from ex-prisoners, carried Canadian war brides to their new homes. We sailed on the 30th and the following day ran into rough seas. The rest of the journey was uneventful and it was a joy to land in Halifax on June 7 at 11:00 p.m. The next day, we boarded a train for Montreal, reaching the city on June 9.

On July 14, approximately five years and three months after my enlistment, I received my discharge and commenced the task of putting my life back together.

It was a relief to be home again and great to be alive.

Barbed-Wire Ballads

The following efforts in verse were written while I was a prisoner-of-war in Germany. Besides being a useful hobby for whiling away the hours and releasing pent-up feelings, they gave me a lasting record of prison life and depict some of a prisoner's feelings and longings.

'MY ALIBI'

To be a poet is no sin,
    It lets come out what is within.
All men feel poetic flame
    But few admit for fear of shame.

Why should man his soul compress
    With secrets deep and unexpressed?
Write your thoughts, release the spring
    Of tumult, deep emotions bring.

(In 'loving' memory of the cells in Düren and the camp at Mühlhausen.)

'FLEE FOUL FLEA'

Where e'er you roam o'er land and sea
   You're sure to find the lowly flea;
In prison camp, no longer free,
    Attack in hordes both you and me
      (We cannot flee).

We inoffensive halt in stride,
   Grab for front, for back or side;
The fleas are gnawing at our hide,
    We must with patience them abide
      (They have no pride).

With powder, spray, rage bitter fight
   Against the pests that itch and bite,
We toss and turn late into night,
    Renew the hunt at dawn's first light
      (With all our might).

From labours we no profit reap,
   In beds and clothes they crawl and creep,
Elude us with a mighty leap;
    We're haggard, worn from lack of sleep
      (Dead on feet).

Alas! They've won the final round;
   Tho' thorough search, cannot be found.
They'll still roam free, in body sound,
    Whilst we lie buried deep in ground
      (Epitaph upon our mound):

   R.I.P.

The fleas have won, it is their boast
   That forced were we to give up ghost.
To fleas I drink this final toast,
    'That you in hell may quickly roast'.

'CAPTIVITY'

Freedom curtailed, 'tis deadly,
 No life for man nor beast;
Take our wealth, pleasures or lives
 But leave us this at least.

'Tis worth far too much, this gift of God,
 For you, mere man, to take;
Make haste, return what you don't own
 Lest you the Lord forsake.

'HEAVEN TO H - - -'

In dreams I scheme
   For ways and means
To hold you in my arms.

At last I grasp
   You in my clasp,
Enfold your lovely charms.

At dawn awake,
   You then forsake
Me to a prison camp.

No longer free,
   Reality
My ardour swiftly damps.

On being recaptured after my first escape attempt, I was lodged in the cells at Arnoldsweiler, near the Belgian border. As I lay on my bunk looking through the bars, a sparrow landed on the sill and looked in at me! In the following verse, I try to describe just how the incident struck me at the time.

'WISE BIRD'

Whilst gazing through these iron bars
   A bird lands on the sill,
With cheery-chirp he greets me
   His eyes with pity fill,
'What sorry plight for you, a man,
   In present day and age
To find yourself so closely cooped,
   Locked up in a cage'.
The humour of this reversed-role
   Strikes me full and true,
My 'wings' are clipped, whilst the bird
   flies free, off into the blue.
Is not this lesson enough for you,
   It is for me at least,
Never again will I encage
   Reptile, bird or beast.

'TO BE OR NOT TO BE?'

Damn oh damn
   I am a man
Why do you doubt my word?

Can't you see
   The shape of me
As pretty as a bird.

I may look sly
   And wink my eye
At boys who pass me by

But can you heal
   The way I feel?
I deeply sigh—'Please try'!

'Tis not my fault
   How earn my salt,
Leave me not forlorn,

When came on earth
   They mixed my birth,
'Twas way that I was born!

(Fortunately, only one amongst thousands!)

'LEST WE FORGET'

Pay grateful tribute in silent prayer
   To efforts of Red Cross;
This life would be a sad affair
   Without them, total loss.

Tho' days seem dreary and so long
   Through darkness shines a ray,
So greet the dawn with smile and song,
   It's parcel issue day.

No reminder is needed for the boys to remember the good
work of the Red Cross Society. Without their parcels, we
would have been sorry-looking objects on our release.

In memory of a comrade, shot and killed whilst attempting escape.

MISADVENTURE

Night falls black and silent, a hush is in the air,
    A dark form tensely crouches, for danger is prepared;
A gentle 'twang', as wire is cut, the form glides silent thro',
    Then suddenly a shot rings out, speeds to its target true.
The dark form now a part of night, silenced for all time;
    He tried and failed, one asks no more, the sacrifice supreme.

'SIREN SONG'

For months on end in England, we'd heard that awful wail,
    Bombs and 'planes came screaming down, like so much rain and hail;
Then to France it followed us, gave out nightly din
    As lay in blacked-out hospital, it sang its song of sin;
And now in far-off Germany, enclosed in prison camp,
    That screeching devil of the night increases in its ramp.

The soldier in the following verse was a prisoner for five long years. He was very popular and adept at many things. One day something snapped—he could endure the waiting no longer.

'UNREASONABLE REASON'

Our comrade's mind is worried,
    Depressed by the long, long wait:
One day he can stand it no longer,
    So calmly walks through the gate.
The guard stands dumbly gaping,
    His wits all dulled by hate;
By the time he sees what's coming off,
    It's just that much too late.

But our comrade's luck just isn't in,
    As he's caught not far from here;
Still bravely makes another dash
    As freedom is so dear.
For his pains he's given many a blow,
    'Til exhausted can stand no more;
Is then returned to his crowded 'home',
    All covered in blood and gore.

Note: This man was taken to hospital for treatment for his injuries, including a bullet wound in his ear. He escaped from custody again and his life ended under the wheels of a moving train.

In England, in 1940, the people huddled in shelters and said, 'We can take it.' In Germany, in 1944–45, the German population said likewise. Anyone being in those two countries during those troublesome times cannot in their hearts truthfully say that a prolonged bombing raid does not in time undermine their morale.

'AIR RAID'

Hideous screech rends silent night,
　With high-pitched wail it sings,
Warns sleeping town of dangerous plight,
　Of swift death borne on wings

That span dark heavens lofty arc
　Whilst nerves are fraught with hideous
Thoughts of horrors stark,
　Torn by roar invidious.

In home no safety can they find;
　Like animals they seek
Dubious security of a kind
　In shelters cold and bleak.

Deep beneath the trembling ground
　They await for their release,
Their breath expelled as hear the sound
　That gives them temporary peace.

'PATIENCE—TOLERANCE'

We who were so impatient within our daily lives
    Have learnt with patience to await wars end and strive
For tolerance with our comrades, so that they in turn
    Will tolerate our habits, different natures come to learn.

When something lacking in our make-up, we acquire it in time,
    Then, if have a virtue, quickly pass it down the line.
These weary years of prison-life have shown each their soul,
    Brought sleeping virtues to the fore, that help attain the goal

Of complete understanding in fellow-men placed in sorry plight
    Who sorely need the comradeship to aid them in the fight
Against the cares of everyday for which we play strange ruse
    To clear the air and help combat those dread 'barbed-wire blues'.

'TRIP-WIRE'

You've heard about the barbed-wire fence
  Keeping prisoners in care
But not of 'trip-wire', stretched so tense;
  Of this you must beware.

To step over is but child's play
  But don't go waste your breath;
It only draws a shot your way
  Which may result in death.

Sign Reads: 'Anyone stepping over this trip-wire will be
shot.'
(The wire is knee-high and approximately twelve feet
from the barbed-wire fences—in between is considered
a 'no-man's land'.)

The examples of comradeship and generosity among a huge body of men who are all in the same sorry plight are well worth mentioning.

'GIVE AND THOU SHALT RECEIVE'

When smile upon your face is seen
   It oft' attracts an answering gleam
From passer-by whom casually met
   Will not admire frown nor fret
As frown mars beauty, lacks of grace,
   Draws scowl alike on other face.

You give of love, for which you earn
   Love tenfold to you in turn.
Hatred changes men to ghouls,
   Transmits itself to other fools.

Of passions, stoop and deeply drink;
   Its returned force welds strongest link.
Give of your seed to pastures ripe;
   New life is born, increase our might
To scatter seed with work-worn hand,
   Enriched by food from yielding land.

Fear, you keep within control
   Or else is felt by other soul.
Make every effort in daily work
   For gold is not for those who shirk.
Hard labour pays with body-strong
   And healthy mind; to do no wrong
Give body food to combat strife:
   The yield is energetic life.

Just giving gives you returned measure
In happiness and heart-felt pleasure.
These things we know, as part of nature,
But yet must learn and then mature
The act of giving worldly goods,
Treasures bought to match our moods.

So hard to part with, things called 'Mine',
'Twas e'er like this since ancient time.
Let's break this habit, learn to give
A mite each day, help others live,
Give when it hurts and then perceive
That what you give, 'Thou Shalt Receive'.

Many things were missed during our enforced imprisonment. All of them were embodied in a longing for our homes in Canada.

'LAND OF MY BIRTH'

I long for a glimpse of my homeland afar,
   Of bright Northern Lights and the twinkling stars,
White blanket of snow mantled over the hills,
   Clean smell of the pines and the gurgle of rills.

Some things are oft' missed and one is the sound
   Of 'scrunch' under heel, of the snow on the ground,
The song of the sleigh-bells, soft music and sweet,
   Keeping time, perfect rhythm to galloping feet.

The cold bite of wind whilst we thrill with the deed
   Of swift flight on skis with incredible speed,
The sight of old friends, welcome smile on their face
   Recall the old memories no one can replace.

The woods in the winter, a fairyland strange,
   Wrapped in deep silence, their grandeur arranged
By God's hand who made them in varying styles
   In majestic aloofness, they stretch endless miles.

Miss crack of the frost in the balsam and spruce,
   The sight of the beaver, magnificent moose,
The glorious maple with gay, coloured leaves
   And gold painted wheat tied so neatly in sheaves.

Oh how I long for the feelings instilled
   With arrival of spring, by new life I am filled,
The soul stirring gladness of first robin's chirp,
   Its throbbing red breast with love song is girt.

The rumbling roar as the river ice flows,
   Rushing torrent of water with volume it grows,
Crushing all in its path as a battering ram
   Soaring high in the air as it's caught in a jam.

The thrill as the snow melts, exposing the earth,
   So grand to remember—a new season's birth,
After long months of winter to climax has come;
   'Tis good once again to feel heat of the sun.

My homeland, my homeland, for you I do crave,
   For 'feel' of your freedom, where no man is slave,
The tales of your history, so enriched with lore,
   The breath-taking vastness of Canada's shores.

'NATURE'S TRICKS'

In this our daily life
    Strange incidents are seen,
The tragic and the comic
    Float 'fore us as a dream:

Men seen sitting brooding,
    Deep frown upon their face;
Others are light-hearted,
    With smile you can't displace.

There's some that we call 'bomb happy',
    Not meaning any harm;
Others have the barbed-wire blues:
    For them, life lost its charm.

There's men who are disfigured,
    Plus others maimed for life;
'Tis pitiful for one to see
    Results of war and strife.

— — —

We've learned our hunger to control
    And try hard to restrain
Our other natural appetites
    From which we must abstain.

The theme of this is 'morals',
    'Gainst which we rage fierce fight;
The ugly acts of some we see
    Cause panic, mental fright.

Unnatural emotions are results
    Of being close confined;
We thank the Lord it's not widespread,
    That most are yet refined.

We'd rather face the foe again,
Be blasted by their mortars,
Than have our 'nature's turn-about'
And land in 'married quarters'!

(Unfortunately, this did occur but wasn't widespread.)

One dreams of strange things when a prisoner. You relive the past, especially the nightmares of bombing. You dream of things that are missing in this life, lights, theatres, the fairer sex and food. The last mentioned is the most vivid. Let me tell you of one of my dreams.

'DREAMS'

I'm eating eggs and bacon or luscious juicy steak,
   Sometimes it's roast brown chicken; I don't know which to take.
And then again there's roast of pork, with apple sauce piled high;
   I close my eyes and munch away, then swallow with a sigh.

The Yorkshire pudding goes down well, along with baked potatoes,
   Drowned in rich brown gravy, with pickles and tomatoes;
Sweet green peas soon follow this and then I have a spell
   To top it off with liver-fried, or lobsters in the shell.

When dessert comes, it's lemon pie with meringue on the crust
   Or apple pie with ice cream to satisfy my lust.
I gorge myself on jellys with whipped-cream inches deep;
   At sight of so much gorgeous food my eyes begin to weep.

The feast I've had is enormous, I'm feeling rather faint;
   The dishes set before me would fill all heaven's saints.
My stomach is distended, my ears begin to ring
   But matter not I'm happy, as happy as a King.

I'm really getting tucked right in, enjoying life in full,
   When suddenly I am awake'd, my blankets roughly pulled;
I'm drooling madly at the mouth and then I start to scream
   As realize just where I am and what I ate—I dreamed!

EXAMPLE OF GERMAN ORDERS POSTED ON BULLETIN BOARDS:

Standing Orders At Kommando 51B

1. Overcoats and caps must behind the bed hang.

2. Mess tins, bottles and boots must on the backside of the bed be hung.

3. House-books must be standing under the beds by the headside.

4. Other things not under the beds.

5. It is allowed something to put in the bed, however, only under the headside and good parts in the middle.

6. The blankets must be put always, properly, up the beds, nothing folds.

7. Up the seams of the walls an only the most unusual object, other things not.

8. The brushes must be hung rights behind the entry.

9. The plate for cigarettes, are always to clean, by leave the room.

10. Beer bottles and others away from the tables, by leave the room.

11. The window boards are everytime free.

12. The latrine seats are always down.

13. After the washing are the hand basins to clean and in one line to put under the bed.

14. Paper and matchen around the barrack, not to throw.

15. The thread—hedge is not to hang with washing and other things, only the park thread into the hedge.

16. Brush by leave the room, also the beds, and clean the tables and cigarette plates.

Signed Kommando Führer
Unteroffizier Hoffman

Order posted at arbeit Kommando, Plothen:

NOTICE

In Germany, the work you produce can be done by a 10 year old boy—if there isn't any change on and from the next Monday, you won't get any paiement at all! It is not like that—you can earn your food and even the treatment will be another. The P.O.W. is treated in Germany as a human creature. The English and French methods are unknown here. If the Englishmen think however, they can be lazy or make a fool of their guards, they are wrong. You can choose either a good production and discipline and in reply for it a good treatment and paiement, or the contrary. A people who claims for himself the name of master of the world, must be able to work. The Poles much better. They really worked and produced a ten times more than you do! This will be my first and last warning.

Signed Ges. Jahn

Verbal orders given at Niederorschel, Thuringen, Kommando 1049, in December, 1942:

First warning by German Interpreter:

'If you refuse to work we will take your stage away from you, also your musical instruments, electric wiring and other privileges.'

Second warning by 'Feldwebel' (Sgt. Major):

'If you refuse to work you will be beaten to work with rifles.'

Third warning by 'Feldwebel':

'If you refuse to work you will be taken out one by one and shot for sabotage.'

German Military HQ notice, posted at Molsdorf—
1/10/1943:

> Prisoners of War are informed that the maximum penalty while attempting to escape, while a Prisoner of War and the killing of a sentry in the attempt, is *30 days solitary confinement*—but if a German or Italian is killed outside the boundary of the P.O.W. camp, the charge will be murder, under civil law.
>
> 'BUT'
>
> British and American P.O.W. are informed that all kinds of violence, also *within the boundarys of the P.O.W. camp*, expecially the killing of a guard while attempting to escape will be punished in conformance with the provisions of article 45 of the Geneva Conventions of 27/7/29 according to German law, that is, *death penalty*, under certain circumstances.
>
> Ober Wehrmacht

Order posted in hospital train en route to Germany via France and Belgium:

> It is forbidden to look through open windows when crossing bridges. It is forbidden to lean out open windows or to wave or signal to the natives. The guards have orders to shoot anyone disobeying these orders.
>
> Signed—Chefartz

Order posted at Molsdorf, Germany, June 13, 1943:

> ### 'WARNING'
>
> In future, any prisoner who escapes in civilian clothing, is liable to be mistaken for a spy or bandit and shot without warning.
>
> Signed Knabu, Hauptmann (Captain)

AIR RAIDS (Comparison)
ENGLAND:

In 1940, air raids were infrequent until August and
September, when the 'blitz' commenced in daylight raids
over all of England, but mainly over the southeast coast,
London and the Midlands. About October, 1940,
the tactics changed to night bombing, which lasted throughout
the winter until the spring of 1941, when raids eased off
to 'nuisance' or 'hit and run' raids, mainly on the
southeast coast. These raids lasted through to 1942 and were
still going strong when we sailed for France in August 1942.

GERMANY:

From August, 1942 to December, 1943, air raids where we
were imprisoned were infrequent. (Excepting for the
time spent in a French hospital in 'Rouen-Sur Seine', where
raids occurred nightly.) Heavy raids in our area of
Thuringen commenced January 1, 1944.

Example Months (1944)	April	46 raids
	May	18 raids
	June	10 raids
	July	17 raids
	August	18 raids
	September	44 raids
	October	25 raids
	November	69 raids
	December	113 raids
Example Months (1945)	January	94 raids
	February	88 raids
	March	179 raids

Example of March, 1945, in Mühlhausen, Thuringen:

Date	Raids	Lasting (Hrs)	(Min.)
March 1	6	6	10
2	8	7	30
3	4	7	
4			
5	6	8	10
6	1	1	50
7	5	5	20
8	3	6	15
9	6	6	35
10	4	6	
11	4	4	10
12	5	5	25
13	4	6	35
14	6	6	
15	7	8	50
16	7	8	45
17	4	6	45
18	5	5	30
19	5	10	55
20	8	8	15
21	6	13	55
22	12	10	40
23	9	9	50
24	11	12	
25	7	10	50
26	8	11	40
27	7	9	45
28	8	8	5
29	2	1	30
30	5	7	10
31	6	16	30

March, 1945 Total Raids—179 Total Time—234 hrs 35 min.

A Note on Photos, Mementos and Artifacts

Group photos of prisoners and photos of military funerals were arranged by the Germans as a means of propaganda to show relatives how well prisoners were treated. Copies of photos were made available to prisoners and were paid for with POW 'script'. Often, new British uniforms would be issued for 'photo use only' and then 'retrieved'. Photos, which were mainly of groups captured at Dunkirk, were later discontinued (military funerals excepted) as prisoners became aware of their propaganda value to the Germans.

Some POW photos and ID cards (*Ausweis*) were acquired after release and were returned to known prisoners who could be located. Others are of European, Polish, Serbian and Russian, etc. POWs. (If any POW recognizes his photo or ID card, he can obtain it by writing to the publisher.)

Some sketches and cartoons are by the author, others were copied from the drawings of various prisoners.

Escape maps were supplied by 'intelligence' through an organization that I prefer not to identify.

ORGANIZED COMPASSION

The International Red Cross played an important role in the lives of prisoners of war, the foremost being the weekly (bombing permitting) supply of Canadian and British food parcels which truly sustained us. If we had to rely on the meagre German rations, our condition would have been as dire as that of the Russian prisoners.

Over and above this most important contribution, the POW camps received musical and sports equipment which helped overcome the daily boredom. Books were another donation but were usually in short supply and generally tattered and worn by the time you got your hands on the more popular ones.

Red Cross representatives from Switzerland also visited the camps to check on conditions in relation to *The Geneva Convention*, but the visits were few and nothing ever developed in response to prisoners' complaints.

The Red Cross also took an active part in the exchange of prisoners. This only involved the DUs (definitely unfit) and only occurred once in our particular camp, Stalag IXC.

All in all, the organization did an excellent job and we, the prisoners, will forever be grateful to it.